Artificial Intelligence

WITHDRAWN

Other Books of Related Interest:

Opposing Viewpoints Series

Biomedical Ethics

Reproductive Technology

Technology and Society

Current Controversies

Online Social Networking

At Issue Series

DNA Databases

Intelligent Design Versus Evolution

Artificial Intelligence

Sylvia Engdahl, Book Editor

GREENHAVEN PRESS

An imprint of Thomson Gale, a part of The Thomson Corporation

Detroit • New York • San Francisco • New Haven, Conn. • Waterville, Maine • London

Christine Nasso, *Publisher*
Elizabeth Des Chenes, *Managing Editor*

© 2008 The Gale Group.

ISBN-13: 978-0-7377-3890-2 (hardcover)
ISBN-10: 0-7377-3890-1 (hardcover)
ISBN-13: 978-0-7377-3891-9 (pbk.)
ISBN-10: 0-7377-3891-X (pbk.)

Library of Congress Control Number: 2007935327

Contents

Chapter 4: AI That Equals or Surpasses Human Intelligence

Foreword

In the news, on the streets, and in neighborhoods, individuals are confronted with a variety of social problems. Such problems may affect people directly: A young woman may struggle with depression, suspect a friend of having bulimia, or watch a loved one battle cancer. And even the issues that do not directly affect her private life—such as religious cults, domestic violence, or legalized gambling—still impact the larger society in which she lives. Discovering and analyzing the complexities of issues that encompass communal and societal realms as well as the world of personal experience is a valuable educational goal in the modern world.

Effectively addressing social problems requires familiarity with a constantly changing stream of data. Becoming well informed about today's controversies is an intricate process that often involves reading myriad primary and secondary sources, analyzing political debates, weighing various experts' opinions—even listening to firsthand accounts of those directly affected by the issue. For students and general observers, this can be a daunting task because of the sheer volume of information available in books, periodicals, on the evening news, and on the Internet. Researching the consequences of legalized gambling, for example, might entail sifting through congressional testimony on gambling's societal effects, examining private studies on Indian gaming, perusing numerous Web sites devoted to Internet betting, and reading essays written by lottery winners as well as interviews with recovering compulsive gamblers. Obtaining valuable information can be time-consuming—since it often requires researchers to pore over numerous documents and commentaries before discovering a source relevant to their particular investigation.

Greenhaven's Contemporary Issues Companion series seeks to assist this process of research by providing readers with useful and pertinent information about today's complex issues. Each volume in this anthology series focuses on a topic of current interest, presenting informative and thought-provoking selections written from a wide variety of viewpoints. The readings selected by the editors include such diverse sources as personal accounts and case studies, pertinent factual and statistical articles, and relevant commentaries and overviews. This diversity of sources and views, found in every Contemporary Issues Companion, offers readers a broad perspective in one convenient volume.

In addition, each title in the Contemporary Issues Companion series is designed especially for young adults. The selections included in every volume are chosen for their accessibility and are expertly edited in consideration of both the reading and comprehension levels of the audience. The structure of the anthologies also enhances accessibility. An introductory essay places each issue in context and provides helpful facts such as historical background or current statistics and legislation that pertain to the topic. The chapters that follow organize the material and focus on specific aspects of the book's topic. Every essay is introduced by a brief summary of its main points and biographical information about the author. These summaries aid in comprehension and can also serve to direct readers to material of immediate interest and need. Finally, a comprehensive index allows readers to efficiently scan and locate content.

The Contemporary Issues Companion series is an ideal launching point for research on a particular topic. Each anthology in the series is composed of readings taken from an extensive gamut of resources, including periodicals, newspapers, books, government documents, the publications of private and public organizations, and Internet Web sites. In these volumes, readers will find factual support suitable for use in reports, debates, speeches, and research papers. The anthologies also facilitate further research, featuring a book and periodical bibliography and a list of organizations to contact for additional information.

A perfect resource for both students and the general reader, Greenhaven's Contemporary Issues Companion series is sure to be a valued source of current, readable information on social problems that interest young adults. It is the editors' hope that readers will find the Contemporary Issues Companion series useful as a starting point to formulate their own opinions about and answers to the complex issues of the present day.

Introduction

To most people, the term *artificial intelligence* refers to artificial beings with human-level minds, often with human-shaped bodies—in other words, to robots of the kind familiar in science fiction. And in fact, both that concept and the word *robot*, which was derived from a Czech word meaning "drudgery," originated in the 1920 play *R.U.R.* by the Czech writer Karel Čapek. In the play, after rebellious robot workers have destroyed the human race, a few of them acquire human emotions, and it is suggested that their progeny will replace humankind. To Čapek, the story was an allegory about the misuse of technology and the exploitation of human workers. But its themes, interpreted more literally, have been common in science fiction ever since—and for decades now, futurists have been seriously discussing the question of whether artificial intelligences will eventually surpass and perhaps supplant humans.

Scientists began studying the possibility of artificial intelligence (AI) in the 1950s, and at first, many believed that intelligent machines could be created relatively soon. It was assumed that the human brain works like a computer and that it would be a straightforward, though difficult, task to duplicate and perhaps improve upon it. Some experts still view AI in this way, maintaining that it is merely a matter of developing sufficiently advanced computer hardware. Others, however, doubt that machines can be given human-level intelligence in the foreseeable future, if ever. The task turned out to be far more complicated than was originally supposed, and many people became disillusioned. Only now is enthusiasm beginning to grow again.

One problem is that although computers can solve very complex problems, often requiring power far surpassing that of a human mind, they cannot yet exhibit as much common sense as a three-year-old child. Children know millions of things, such as "the sky is blue" and "people generally sleep at night," that are so obvious that it is difficult if not impossible to define them all—yet for a computer to "know" them, they would have to be entered as data, one at a time. This has been tried, but so far it has proved impractical to build a large enough database. No computer is able interpret a simple children's story, let alone deal with new situations that require a background of general knowledge comparable to an adult's. Furthermore, even the most advanced supercomputers cannot do what any small child can do when shown a picture: They cannot tell the difference between a cat and a dog.

Another problem is that no one really knows how the human mind works. There are many theories about the brain, but scientists are still a long way from understanding it. Merely duplicating the physical structure of the brain might not be enough to produce a thinking mind—although many researchers believe it would—and it is not yet possible to try it and see. It may turn out that factors that have not even been imagined are involved.

Meanwhile, although not much progress has been made toward generalized machine intelligence, a great deal of "intelligent" software has been produced to accomplish specific tasks. A computer has beaten a human world chess champion, for instance. And far more prevalent than feats like this are the many forms of AI that have been incorporated into people's daily lives. Most of these—such as airline reservation systems, e-mail spam filters, and tools to help teachers grade papers—are not considered AI by the public. "As soon as we solve a problem," says Martha Pollack, a professor at the Artificial Intelligence Laboratory at the University of Michigan, "instead of looking at the solution as AI, we come to view it as just another computer system."

Development of robots has also proceeded, not robots with general intelligence or self-awareness, but simpler ones for special uses, from vacuum cleaners and pet dogs to Mars landers. Some of today's robots have human shape. The AI required by these nonthinking robots is more complex than it may appear to be; just getting a humanoid robot to walk on uneven ground is a major undertaking.

Theorists often make a distinction between "Weak AI" and "Strong AI." Weak AI includes the use of computer technology for narrow, specialized tasks that do not require the full range of human cognitive abilities. Strong AI, in contrast, refers to machines that approach or exceed human intelligence in a more general sense and are to some degree self-aware. Will the creation of Strong AI ever be possible? That is a controversial issue. Some experts believe it will. One of the leading advocates of this view is Ray Kurzweil, who is sure that it will happen by 2029. Others believe it will take much longer, or that it will never happen at all. People who believe understanding the human mind is just a matter of figuring out how the brain works are more apt to think human-level AI will be created than are those who believe there is more to the mind than brain circuitry.

Among scientists who do believe in Strong AI, there has been a great deal of discussion about what impact its development will have on human society. "Some people assume that being intelligent is basically the same as having human mentality," says computer expert Jeff Hawkins in his book *On Intelligence*. "They fear that intelligent machines will resent being 'enslaved' because humans hate being enslaved. They fear that intelligent machines will try to take over the world because intelligent people throughout history have tried to take over the world. But these fears rest on a false analogy. They are based on a conflation of intelligence—the neocortical algorithm—with the emotional drives of the old brain—things like fear, paranoia, and desire. But intelligent machines will not have . . . anything resembling human emotion unless we painstakingly design them to."

Unlike Hawkins, many researchers believe that actual minds similar to human minds will spontaneously emerge when artificially constructed brains become complex enough to have human intelligence. According to this view, that is how human consciousness arose in the first place; thus there is no reason to think it would not happen again. Not everyone, however, agrees with this theory of the human mind's origin. In addition to people who base their beliefs on religion, there are experts who feel that mere brain complexity cannot sufficiently explain self-awareness or emotion. Some, such as Roger Penrose, whose controversial book *The Emperor's New Mind* caused a stir in 1989, believe that quantum mechanics plays an essential role in consciousness and that computers therefore cannot simulate it.

If intelligent machines do come into existence, the issue of whether they will be friendly or hostile to humans is obviously an important one, so important that believers in Strong AI argue that it should be carefully considered beforehand. What steps can be taken, they ask, to ensure that artificial intelligences will be friendly? Some fear that nothing can do so, since AIs that were smarter than humans could not be controlled. Some even think that for superior machines to succeed, biological intelligence is the natural next step in history and would not be a bad thing.

Still another issue receiving attention is whether machines with human intelligence would be entitled to the same rights as humans. In fact, some people take this so seriously that in 2006 a report about future technology commissioned by the British government dealt with it, drawing numerous comments from the media. According to the report, said the BBC News, if such rights were granted, "countries would be obliged to provide social benefits including housing and even 'robo-healthcare,'" while "robots would have certain responsibilities such as voting, the obligation to pay taxes, and perhaps serving compulsory military service." Scientists dismissed these speculations as premature. Noel Sharkey, a computer scientist at the University of Sheffield, said, "The idea of machine consciousness and rights is a distraction, it's fairy tale stuff. We need proper informed debate, about the public safety for instance of the millions of domestic robots that are predicted to be arriving in the next few years."

CHAPTER 1

Artificial Intelligence Today

Renewed Enthusiasm for Artificial Intelligence

Economist

The Economist *is a major weekly newsmagazine published in London but distributed internationally; about half the copies are sold in North America. Its articles do not carry bylines. In the following viewpoint, the author explains that although there were high hopes for the development of artificial intelligence (AI) during the 1980s, a backlash occurred when thinking computers and household robots failed to materialize. Researchers began to avoid the term; whenever "smart" computer programs were developed, they were called something else. Now, in the twenty-first century, the concept of artificial intelligence is gaining favor again. But now, expectations are not as high as they were when the public envisioned the creation of intelligent, conscious computers such as HAL in the movie* 2001: A Space Odyssey. *Today, people are judging AI by what it can actually do instead of by ideas based on science fiction.*

After years in the wilderness, the term "artificial intelligence" seems poised to make a comeback.

Like big hairdos and dubious pop stars, the term "artificial intelligence" (AI) was big in the 1980s, vanished in the 1990s—and now seems to be attempting a comeback. The term reentered public consciousness most dramatically with the release [in 2001] of "A.I.", a movie about a robot boy. But the term is also being rehabilitated within the computer industry. Researchers, executives and marketing people are using the expression without irony or inverted commas [quotation marks].

And it is not always hype. The term is being applied, with some justification, to products that depend on technology that was originally cooked up by AI researchers. Admittedly, the comeback has a long way to go, and some firms still prefer to avoid the phrase. But the fact that others are starting to use it again suggests that AI is no longer simply regarded as an over-ambitious and underachieving field of research.

That field was launched, and the term "artificial intelligence" coined, at a conference in 1956 by a group of researchers that included Marvin Minsky, John McCarthy, Herbert Simon and Alan Newell, all of whom went on to become leading lights in the subject. The term provided a sexy-sounding but informative semantic umbrella for a research programme that encompassed such previously disparate fields as operations research, cybernetics, logic and computer science. The common strand was an attempt to capture or mimic human abilities using machines. That said, different groups of researchers attacked different problems, from speech recognition to chess playing, in different ways; AI unified the field in name only. But it was a term that captured the public's imagination.

Most researchers agree that the high-water mark for AI occurred around 1985. A public reared on science-fiction movies and excited by the growing power of home computers had high expectations. For years, AI researchers had implied that a breakthrough was just around the corner. ("Within a generation the problem of creating 'artificial intelligence' will be substantially solved," Dr Minsky said in 1967.) Prototypes of medical-diagnosis programs, speech recognition software and expert systems appeared to be making progress. The 1985 conference of the American Association of Artificial Intelligence (AAAI) was, recalls Eric Horvitz, now a researcher at Microsoft, attended by thousands of people, including many interested members of the public and entrepreneurs looking for the next big thing.

It proved to be a false dawn. Thinking computers and household robots failed to materialise, and a backlash ensued. "There was undue optimism," says David Leake, a researcher at Indiana University who is also the editor of *AI Magazine*, which is published by the AAAI. "When people realised these were hard problems, there was retrenchment. It was good for the field, because people started looking for approaches that involved less hubris." By the late 1980s, the term AI was being eschewed by many researchers, who preferred instead to align themselves with specific sub-disciplines such as neural networks, agent technology, case-based reasoning, and so on. The expectations of the early 1980s, says Dr Horvitz, "created a sense that the term itself was overblown. It's a phrase that captures a long-term dream, but it implicitly promises a lot. For a variety of reasons, people pulled back from using it."

Ironically, in some ways, AI was a victim of its own success. Whenever an apparently mundane problem was solved, such as building a system that could land an aircraft unattended, or read handwritten postcodes to speed mail sorting, the problem was deemed not to have been AI in the first place. "If it works, it can't be AI," as Dr Leake characterises it. The effect of repeatedly moving the goal-posts in this way was that AI came to refer to bluesky research that was still years away from commercialisation. Researchers joked that AI stood for "almost implemented". Meanwhile, the technologies that worked well enough to make it on to the market, such as speech recognition, language translation and decision-support software, were no longer regarded as AI. Yet all three once fell well within the umbrella of AI research.

Quiet Respectability

But the tide may now be turning. "There was a time when companies were reluctant to say 'we're doing or using AI', but that's now changing," says Dr Leake. A number of start-ups are touting their use of AI technology. Predictive Networks of Cambridge, Massachusetts, focuses advertising using "artificial intelligence-based Digital Silhouettes" that analyse customer behaviour. The firm was founded by Devin Hosea, a former National Science Foundation fellow in artificial intelligence.

Another firm, HNC Software of San Diego, whose backers include the Defence Advanced Research Project Agency in Washington, DC, reckons that its new approach to neural networks based on a cluster of 30 Pentium processors is the most powerful and promising approach to artificial intelligence ever discovered. HNC claims that its system could be used to spot camouflaged vehicles on a battlefield or extract a voice signal from a noisy background—tasks humans can do well, but computers cannot. Whether or not its technology lives up to the claims made for it, that HNC is emphasising the use of AI is itself an interesting development.

Large companies are also using the term. Dr Leake points out that Bill Gates of Microsoft gave the keynote speech at [2001's] AAAI conference and demonstrated several Microsoft technologies that are close to being incorporated into the company's products. [In late 2001,] Microsoft trumpeted a "breakthrough application that enlists the power of artificial intelligence to help users manage mobile communications."

The product in question is Mobile Manager, which uses Dr Horvitz's research into Bayesian decision-making to decide which e-mail messages in an individual's in-box are important enough to forward to a pager. Dr Horvitz says he is happy to refer to his work as AI. His current work, which involves using spare computing capacity to anticipate and prepare for the user's most likely next action, is based on research published in *Artificial Intelligence*. "We just submitted a paper on how a theorem-proving program could exploit uncertainty to run more efficiently," he says. "That's core AI. I personally feel better about using the term. There are people, myself and others, who use the term proudly."

Sony also unabashedly uses the term AI when referring to its robot dog, AIBO. (The name is derived from the combination of "AI" and "bot", and means companion in Japanese.)

The company boasts that "advanced artificial intelligence gives AIBO the ability to make its own decisions while maturing over time." It sounds like hype, though once you have seen an AIBO's uncannily life-like behaviour, the AI label seems appropriate. AIBO's intelligence, such as it is, relies on genetic algorithms, another trick that has been dug out from the AI toolkit.

In computer gaming, the term AI has always been used with a straight face. The gaming community got interested in AI in the late 1980s when personal computers started to get more powerful, says Steven Woodcock, a programmer who has worked in both the defence and games industries, and who maintains a website devoted to the study of AI in gaming: www.gameai.com. As graphics improve, he says, a game "needs other discriminators, like whether it plays smart." Game reviews routinely refer to the quality of the AI—well, what else would you call it?—and some games are renowned for the lifelike quality of their computer opponents.

Mr Woodcock says there is now quite a lot of traffic in both directions between AI programmers in the academic and gaming worlds. Military simulators, he notes, are increasingly based on games, and games programmers are good at finding quick-and-dirty ways to implement AI techniques that will make computer opponents more engagingly lifelike. Gaming has also helped to advertise and popularise AI in the form of such impressive games as "The Sims", "Black & White" and "Creatures".

Information Overload

Another factor that may boost the prospects for AI is the demise of the dotcoms. Investors are now looking for firms using clever technology, rather than just a clever business model, to differentiate themselves. In particular, the problem of information overload, exacerbated by the growth of e-mail and the explosion in the number of web pages, means there are plenty of opportunities for new technologies to help filter and categorise information—classic AI problems. That may mean that artificial-intelligence start-ups—thin on the ground since the early 1980s—will start to emerge, provided they can harness the technology to do something useful. But if they can, there will be no shortage of buzzwords for the marketing department.

Not everyone is rushing to embrace this once-stigmatised term, however. IBM, for example, is working on self-healing, self-tuning systems that are more resilient to failure and require less human intervention than existing computers. Robert Morris, director of IBM's Almaden Research Centre in Silicon Valley, admits this initiative, called "autonomic computing", borrows ideas from AI research. But, he says, where AI is about getting computers to solve problems that would be solved in the frontal lobe of the brain, autonomic computing has more in common with the autonomic nervous system. To some extent, he suggests, the term AI has outgrown its usefulness. He notes that it was always a broad, fuzzy term, and encompassed some fields whose practitioners did not regard their work as AI. And while IBM continues to conduct research into artificial intelligence, Dr Morris does not link autonomic computing to such work. "This stuff is real," he says.

Similarly, Max Thiercy, head of development at Albert, a French firm that produces natural-language search software, also avoids the term AI. "I consider the term a bit obsolete," he says. "It can make our customers frightened." This seems odd, because the firm's search technology uses a classic AI technique, applying multiple algorithms to the same data, and then evaluates the results to see which approach was most effective. Even so, the firm prefers to use such terms as "natural language processing" and "machine learning".

Perhaps the biggest change in AI's fortunes is simply down to the change of date. The film *A.I.* was based on an idea by the late director Stanley Kubrick, who also dealt with the topic in another film, *2001: A Space Odyssey*, which was released in 1969. *2001* featured an intelligent computer called HAL 9000 with a hypnotic speaking voice. As well as understanding and speaking English, HAL could play chess and even learned to lip-read. HAL thus encapsulated the optimism of the 1960s that intelligent computers would be widespread by 2001.

But 2001 has been and gone, and there is still no sign of a HAL-like computer. Individual systems can play chess or transcribe speech, but a general theory of machine intelligence remains elusive. It may be, however, that now that 2001 turned out to be just another year on the calendar, the comparison with HAL no longer seems quite so important, and AI can now be judged by what it can do, rather than by how well it matches up to a 30-year-old science-fiction film. "People are beginning to realise that there are impressive things that these systems can do," says Dr Leake hopefully. "They're no longer looking for HAL."

The Variety of Present-Day Robots

Duncan Graham-Rowe

Duncan Graham-Rowe is a writer for New Scientist *magazine. In the following selection he describes the kinds of robots that currently exist or are planned for the near future. Advances in the field of artificial intelligence (AI) have recently made it possible to create useful ones, some of which are selling well to the public—not only household robots such as vacuum cleaners, but robo-pets meant for entertainment. Robotic vehicles and planes are now being built, and robotic tools are used by surgeons. But there are still many challenging problems to be solved in the field of robotics.*

Ever since the Czech writer Karel Čapek first coined the term "robot" in 1921, there has been an expectation that robots would some day deliver us from the drudgery of hard work. The word—from the Czech "robota", for hard labour and servitude—described intelligent machines used as slaves in his play *R.U.R.* (*Rossum's Universal Robots*).

Today, over one million household robots, and a further 1.1 million industrial robots, are operating worldwide. Robots are used to perform tasks that require great levels of precision or are simply repetitive and boring. Many also do jobs that are hazardous to people, such as exploring shipwrecks, helping out after disasters, studying other planets and defusing bombs or mines.

Robots are increasingly marching into our lives. In the future, robots will act as carers, medics, bionic enhancements, companions, entertainers, security guards, traffic police and even soldiers.

Domestic Invasion

Despite the longevity of the robot concept, robotic butlers that roam our homes and relieve us from housework still seemed far from reality until very recently. Instead, the vast majority of robots worked in factories performing the industrial functions of brainless machines.

However, a combination of increased computing power and advances made in the field of artificial intelligence, or AI, have now made software smart enough to make robots considerably more useful.

A recent report published by the United Nations revealed that sales of domestic robots had tripled in a single year. What's more, they were well on their way to outstripping their industrial cousins.

While a large portion of the household robots were made up of robotic vacuum cleaners, mops, lawn mowers, pool cleaners, security bots and even robotic baby-rockers—the real boom was in entertainment robots.

Suddenly people were happy to pay for robots that had no specific functional value. Instead these bots, such as Sony's Aibo robotic dog and its robo-pups served as robo-pets and companions, rather than slaves.

This is partly because many domestic chores still pose a real challenge for robots, in terms of dexterity and intelligence, even with seemingly simple chores such as ironing.

Movers and Shakers

Away from the domestic front, the modern bot can take many other forms. Some are even designed to change their form, such as shape-shifting tetrabots or self-cloning robots.

And while we often think of robots being humanoid, such as Honda's Asimo and Sony's Qrio, there is as much interest, if not more, in emulating other creatures like insects, lobsters, orang-utans, alligators, snakes and fish. A robot guard dragon has even been created.

Whether they have two legs, many legs, or no legs at all, considerable advances have been made in robot locomotion, including bipedal walking, rambling, crawling, rock-climbing, bouncing, slithering and swimming.

There are also wheeled bots that work as autonomous vehicles, such as the desert racers that compete in the DARPA [Defense Advanced Research Projects Agency] Grand Challenge to be the fastest to cross a desert without any human control.

Robot Wars

One area where even more advances in autonomy have been made is the development of unmanned aerial vehicles, or UAVs. These are essentially remotely-controlled spy planes that are capable of flying themselves if they lose contact with their pilot. These planes can also be used to monitor forest fires. Some robots have even learnt to fly of their own accord.

The Pentagon has started arming some UAVs, making them capable of responding with firepower against aggressive attacks—so-called unmanned combat vehicles, or UCVs. Robots that act as battlefield spies have also been designed.

Also aiming to remove humans from dangerous situations are space agencies, such as NASA, who have developed many space exploration robots. For example, the robonaut is a remotely-operated robot, designed to perform dangerous space walks in the place of an astronaut.

In addition, NASA has already sent robotic rovers to Mars, developed robotic dirt scoopers, "flying eyes" and probes for interplanetary exploration and even sent droids off to try to explore asteroids. Space probes such as Huygens, which landed on Titan, and Russia's Venera 9, which landed on Venus, are sometimes considered robots too.

And it's not just other planets that robots are good for exploring. Robotic submarines, also known as remotely operated vehicles, or ROVs, have now become an important way of exploring the deep ocean or ice-capped waters, while heat resistant robots are now used to patrol and monitor the activity in volcanoes. A robotic rover has even been used to explore Egyptian pyramids.

Precision Surgeons

Operating on the human body requires high skill but also great control, something robots can provide. The idea of robotic surgery prompted early fears of unsupervised robots let loose to operate, but the reality is that robots now assist surgeons to perform precision procedures.

The most successful of these is arguably the da Vinci robotic surgical system, which is used for keyhole surgery, to operate on anything from gall bladder removals and brain surgery to heart bypasses.

Similarly, tiny, wireless and robotic camera-capsules have been used diagnostically, by allowing them to pass through a patient's digestive system. Others have been designed to move about by remote control in the abdominal cavity, beaming images back to the surgeon, or even taking biopsy samples. Robot hands have even been developed to scan for breast cancer.

Such life-saving robots have proved so successful that dentists are considering using a robotic dental drill to make implant dental surgery cheaper, quicker and, crucially, less painful.

Actuators and Sensors

But despite all the successes, there are still many challenges in robotics. These include producing better actuators (which control how robots move), sensors (which allow them to detect their environment) and ultimately making bots much smarter.

Current motors, and hydraulic or pneumatic actuators, are either too weak, or too bulky and noisy. Artificial muscle might be one solution, but so far these have failed to be strong enough to beat even a teenage girl in a robotic arm wrestling match.

Bipedal and humanoid robots have proved a particular problem. Robots on wheels, or those that move like insects, have found it much easier to balance and get around.

And while much early research in robotics focused on using sonar sensors because they were cheap and easy to use, the focus today is on the more challenging, yet richer, vision-based navigation systems.

Similarly, while there is much research on making robotic arms and hands, the difficulty lies in making electronic skin sensitive enough to detect fragile or slippery objects by touch alone. A robot that mimics human speech is also under development.

To encourage advances in these all these fields, it is now common for the robotic community to use contests. These include baseball catching contests, to improve dexterity; goldfish-catching contests, to improve underwater manoeuverability; even robotic camel jockeying contests have been held, though they were created to replace child jockeys.

The ultimate test perhaps is robot soccer. This is driving development in just about every area of robotics from the ability to run and kick a ball to communicating and demonstrating teamwork. The grand aim is to have a team of humanoid robots that can beat the best human soccer team in the world by 2050.

Until then the question remains that if robots are ever made smart enough to do our ironing will they also be smart enough to refuse to do it for us? Would we suddenly have a robotic-rebellion on our hands?

A New Generation of Robots in Japan

Anthony Faiola

Anthony Faiola is a staff writer for the Washington Post. *In the following selection he describes the popularity of consumer robots in Japan, where they are more widely accepted than in the United States. Although American scientists are as advanced in robotics as the Japanese, they have concentrated on military applications, whereas the Japanese are investing billions of dollars in robots aimed at altering daily life. Some Japanese scientists believe that the use of robots will change human lifestyles even more than computers or cell phones did. In Japan, robot receptionists, night watchmen, and hospital workers are already employed, and robotic pets are common, including robotic baby seals that are loved by lonely elderly people in nursing homes.*

Ms. Saya, a perky receptionist in a smart canary-yellow suit, beamed a smile from behind the "May I Help You?" sign on her desk, offering greetings and answering questions posed by visitors at a local university. But when she failed to welcome a workman who had just walked by, a professor stormed up to Saya and dished out a harsh reprimand.

"You're so stupid!" said the professor, Hiroshi Kobayashi, towering over her desk.

"Eh?" she responded, her face wrinkling into a scowl. "I tell you, I am not stupid!"

Truth is, Saya isn't even human. But in a country where robots are changing the way people live, work, play and even love, that doesn't stop Saya the cyber-receptionist from defending herself from men who are out of line. With voice recognition technology allowing 700 verbal responses and an almost infinite number of facial expressions from joy to despair, surprise to rage, Saya may not be biological—but she is nobody's fool.

"I almost feel like she's a real person," said Kobayashi, an associate professor at the Tokyo University of Science and Saya's inventor. Having worked at the university for almost two years now, she's an old hand at her job. "She has a temper . . . and she sometimes makes mistakes, especially when she has low energy," the professor said.

Consumer Robots Are Common in Japan

Saya's wrath is the latest sign of the rise of the robot. Analysts say Japan is leading the world in rolling out a new generation of consumer robots. Some scientists are calling the wave a technological force poised to change human lifestyles more radically than the advent of the computer or the cell phone.

Though perhaps years away in the United States, this long-awaited, as-seen-on-TV world—think *The Jetsons* or *Blade Runner*—is already unfolding in Japan, with robots now used as receptionists, night watchmen, hospital workers, guides, pets and more. The onslaught of new robots led the government last month to establish a committee to draw up safety guidelines for the keeping of robots in homes and offices. Officials compiled a report in January predicting that every household in Japan will own at least one robot by 2015, perhaps sooner.

Scientists and government authorities . . . dubbed 2005 the unofficial "year of the robot," with humans . . . interacting with their electronic spawn as never before at the 2005 World Expo opening just outside the city of Nagoya on March 25. At the 430-acre site, 15 million visitors . . . [mingled] with some of the most highly developed examples of Japanese artificial intelligence, many of which are already on sale. . . .

Greeting visitors in four languages and guiding them to their desired destinations . . . [was] Mitsubishi Heavy Industries' yellow midget robot, Wakamaru. A trio of humanoid robots by Sony, Toyota and Honda . . . [were] dancing and playing musical instruments at the opening ceremony. Parents visiting the World Expo . . . [could] leave their children in the care of a robotic babysitter—NEC's PaPeRo—which recognizes individual children's faces and can notify parents by cell phone in case of emergency.

Also on display: a wheelchair robot now being deployed by the southern city of Kitakyushu that independently navigates traffic crossings and sidewalks using a global positioning and integrated circuit chip system. In June, Expo visitors . . . [could] enter a robot room—a more distant vision of the future where by 2020 merely speaking a word from your sofa will open the refrigerator door, allowing your personal robot assistant to deliver the cold beverage of your choice.

Robots Are Changing Japanese Society

"We have reached the point in Japan of a major breakthrough in the use of robot technology and our society is changing as a result," said Kazuya Abe, a top official at NEDO, the national institute in charge of coordinating science research and development. "People are and will be living alongside robots, which are seen here as more than just machines. This is all about AI"—artificial intelligence, Abe said—"about the creation of something that is not human, but can be a complement or companion to humans in society. That future is happening here now."

While employing a measure of new technology, many such robots are envisioned merely as new interfaces—more user-friendly means of combining existing ways of accessing the Internet or reaching loved ones through cell phone networks.

In the quest for artificial intelligence, the United States is perhaps just as advanced as Japan. But analysts stress that the focus in the United States has been largely on military applications. By contrast, the Japanese government, academic institutions and major corporations are investing billions of dollars on consumer robots aimed at altering everyday life, leading to an earlier dawn of what many here call the "age of the robot."

But the robotic rush in Japan is also being driven by unique societal needs. Confronting a major depopulation problem due to a record low birthrate and its status as the nation with the longest lifespan on Earth, Japanese are fretting about who will staff the factory floors of the world's second-largest economy in the years ahead. Toyota, Japan's biggest automaker, has come up with one answer in moving to create a line of worker robots with human-like hands able to perform multiple sophisticated tasks.

With Japanese youth shying from so-called 3-K jobs—referring to the Japanese words for labor that is dirty, dangerous or physically taxing—Alsok, the nation's second-largest security guard company, has developed a line of robo-cops. The guard robots, one version of which is already being used by a client in southern Japan, can detect and thwart intruders using sensors and paint guns. They can also put out fires and spot water leaks.

It is perhaps no surprise that robots would find their first major foothold in Japan. Japanese dolls and toys, including a moving crab using clockwork technology dating to the 1800s, are considered by some to be among the first robots. Rather than the monstrous Terminators of American movies, robots here are instead seen as gentle, even idealistic creatures epitomized by *Astroboy*, the 1960s Japanese cartoon about an electronic kid with a big heart.

"In Western countries, humanoid robots are still not very accepted, but they are in Japan," said Norihiro Hagita, director of the ATR Intelligent Robotics and Communication Laboratories in Keihanna Science City near Kyoto. "One reason is religion. In Japanese [Shinto] religion, we believe that all things have gods within them. But in Western countries, most people believe in only one God. For us, however, a robot can have an energy all its own."

A Robotic Baby Seal Helps the Elderly

A case in point is the Paro—a robotic baby harp seal, developed with $10 million in government grants, that went on sale commercially this month for $3,500 each. All 200 units sold out in less than 50 hours.

The seal is meant to provide therapy for the elderly who are filling Japanese nursing homes at an alarming rate while often falling prey to depression and loneliness.

With 30 sensors, the seal begins over time to recognize its master's voice and hand gestures. It coos and flaps its furry white down in delight at gentle nuzzles, but squeals in anger when handled roughly.

Researchers have been testing the robot's effect on the elderly at a nursing home in Tsukuba, about 40 miles northeast of Tokyo. During a recent visit by a reporter, the sad eyes of elderly residents lit up as the two resident robot seals were brought out. Tests have shown that the cute newcomers indeed reduce stress and depression among the elderly. Just ask Sumi Kasuya, 89, who cradled a seal robot while singing it a lullaby on a recent afternoon.

"I have no grandchildren and my family does not come to see me very often," said Kasuya, clutching fast to the baby seal robot wiggling in her arms. "So I have her," she said, pointing to the seal. "She is so cute, and is always happy to see me."

Using Robots Raises Safety Concerns

Economist

The Economist *is a major weekly newsmagazine published in London but distributed internationally; about half the copies are sold in North America. Its articles do not carry bylines. The author of the following selection discusses growing safety concerns over the use of robots by factory workers and consumers. Robot experts met in 2006 to consider whether special regulations are needed to ensure that robots are safe. As robots become capable of learning on their own, it will become impossible to fully predict their behavior. Although all products are designed to minimize the risk of their causing injury, accidents still happen, and the same will be true with robots. The issue is likely to give rise to lawsuits; if an intelligent robot causes harm, can its designer be held responsible? Furthermore, in addition to posing physical danger, robots might prove dangerous to humans by bringing out their worst aspects—for example, kicking a robot dog might make someone more likely to kick a real one.*

As robots move into homes and offices, ensuring that they do not injure people will be vital. But how?

In 1981 Kenji Urada, a 37-year-old Japanese factory worker, climbed over a safety fence at a Kawasaki plant to carry out some maintenance work on a robot. In his haste, he failed to switch the robot off properly. Unable to sense him, the robot's powerful hydraulic arm kept on working and accidentally pushed the engineer into a grinding machine. His death made Urada the first recorded victim to die at the hands of a robot.

This gruesome industrial accident would not have happened in a world in which robot behaviour was governed by the Three Laws of Robotics drawn up by Isaac Asimov, a science-fiction writer. The laws appeared in *I, Robot,* a book of short stories published in 1950 that inspired a recent Hollywood film. But decades later the laws, designed to prevent robots from harming people either through action or inaction . . . remain in the realm of fiction.

Indeed, despite the introduction of improved safety mechanisms, robots have claimed many more victims since 1981. Over the years people have been crushed, hit on the head, welded and even had molten aluminium poured over them by robots. [In 2005] there were 77 robot-related accidents in Britain alone, according to the Health and Safety Executive [a U.K. government agency].

With robots now poised to emerge from their industrial cages and to move into homes and workplaces, roboticists are concerned about the safety implications beyond the factory floor. To address these concerns, leading robot experts have come together to try to find ways to prevent robots from harming people. Inspired by the Pugwash Conferences—an international group of scientists, academics and activists founded in 1957 to campaign for the non-proliferation of nuclear weapons—the new group of robo-ethicists met earlier this year [2006] in Genoa, Italy, and announced their initial findings in March at the European Robotics Symposium in Palermo, Sicily.

Security, Safety, and Sex

"Security, safety and sex are the big concerns," says Henrik Christensen, chairman of the European Robotics Network at the Swedish Royal Institute of Technology in Stockholm, and one of the organisers of the new robo-ethics group. Should robots that are strong enough or heavy enough to crush people be allowed into homes? Is "system malfunction" a justifiable defence for a robotic fighter plane that contravenes the Geneva Convention and mistakenly fires on innocent civilians? And should robotic sex dolls resembling children be legally allowed?

These questions may seem esoteric but in the next few years they will become increasingly relevant, says Dr Christensen. According to the United Nations Economic Commission for Europe's World Robotics Survey, in 2002 the number of domestic and service robots more than tripled, nearly outstripping their industrial counterparts. By the end of 2003 there were more than 600,000 robot vacuum cleaners and lawn mowers—a figure predicted to rise to more than 4m [4 thousand] by the end of next year. Japanese industrial firms are racing to build humanoid robots to act as domestic helpers for the elderly, and South Korea has set a goal that 100% of households should have domestic robots by 2020. In light of all this, it is crucial that we start to think about safety and ethical guidelines now, says Dr Christensen.

Stop Right There

So what exactly is being done to protect us from these mechanical menaces? "Not enough," says Blay Whitby, an artificial-intelligence expert at the University of Sussex in England. This is hardly surprising given that the field of "safety-critical computing" is barely a decade old, he says. But things are changing, and researchers are increasingly taking an interest in trying to make robots safer. One approach, which sounds simple enough, is try to program them to avoid contact with people altogether. But this is much harder than it sounds. Getting a robot to navigate across a cluttered room is difficult enough without having to take into account what its various limbs or appendages might bump into along the way.

Regulating the behaviour of robots is going to become more difficult in future, since they will increasingly have self-learning mechanisms built into them, says Gianmarco Veruggio, a roboticist at the Institute of Intelligent Systems for Automation in Genoa, Italy. As a result, their behaviour will become impossible to predict fully, he says, since they will not be behaving in predefined ways but will learn new behaviour as they go.

Then there is the question of unpredictable failures. What happens if a robot's motors stop working, or it suffers a system failure just as it is performing heart surgery or handing you a cup of hot coffee? You can, of course, build in redundancy by adding backup systems, says Hirochika Inoue, a veteran roboticist at the University of Tokyo who is now an adviser to the Japan Society for the Promotion of Science. But this guarantees nothing, he says. "One hundred per cent safety is impossible through technology," says Dr Inoue. This is because ultimately no matter how thorough you are, you cannot anticipate the unpredictable nature of human behaviour, he says. Or to put it another way, no matter how sophisticated your robot is at avoiding people, people might not always manage to avoid it, and could end up tripping over it and falling down the stairs.

Legal Problems

So where does this leave Asimov's Three Laws of Robotics? They were a narrative device, and were never actually meant to work in the real world, says Dr Whitby. Quite apart from the fact that the laws require the robot to have some form of human-like intelligence, which robots still lack, the laws themselves don't actually work very well. Indeed, Asimov repeatedly knocked them down in his robot stories, showing time and again how these seemingly watertight rules could produce unintended consequences.

In any case, says Dr Inoue, the laws really just encapsulate commonsense principles that are already applied to the design of most modern appliances, both domestic and industrial. Every toaster, lawn mower and mobile phone is designed to minimise the risk of causing injury—yet people still manage to electrocute themselves, lose fingers or fall out of windows in an effort to get a better signal. At the very least, robots must meet the rigorous safety standards that cover existing products. The question is whether new, robot-specific rules are needed—and, if so, what they should say.

"Making sure robots are safe will be critical," says Colin Angle of iRobot, which has sold over 2m [2 thousand] "Roomba" household-vacuuming robots. But he argues that his firm's robots are, in fact, much safer than some popular toys. "A radio-controlled car controlled by a six-year old is far more dangerous than a Roomba," he says. If you tread on a Roomba, it will not cause you to slip over; instead, a rubber pad on its base grips the floor and prevents it from moving. "Existing regulations will address much of the challenge," says Mr Angle. "I'm not yet convinced that robots are sufficiently different that they deserve special treatment."

Robot safety is likely to surface in the civil courts as a matter of product liability. "When the first robot carpet-sweeper sucks up a baby, who will be to blame?" asks John Hallam, a professor at the University of Southern Denmark in Odense. If a robot is autonomous and capable of learning, can its designer be held responsible for all its actions? Today the answer to these questions is generally "yes". But as robots grow in complexity it will become a lot less clear cut, he says.

"Right now, no insurance company is prepared to insure robots," says Dr Inoue. But that will have to change, he says. Last month [May 2006] Japan's ministry of trade and industry announced a set of safety guidelines for home and office robots. They will be required to have sensors to help them avoid collisions with humans; to be made from soft and light materials to minimise harm if a collision does occur; and to have an emergency shut-off button. This was largely prompted by a big robot exhibition held last summer, which made the authorities realise that there are safety implications when thousands of people are not just looking at robots, but mingling with them, says Dr Inoue.

However, the idea that general-purpose robots, capable of learning, will become widespread is wrong, suggests Mr Angle.

It is more likely, he believes, that robots will be relatively dumb machines designed for particular tasks. Rather than a humanoid robot maid, "it's going to be a heterogeneous swarm of robots that will take care of the house," he says.

Robots Might Affect How Humans Behave

Probably the area of robotics that is likely to prove most controversial is the development of robotic sex toys, says Dr Christensen. "People are going to be having sex with robots in the next five years," he says. Initially these robots will be pretty basic, but that is unlikely to put people off, he says. "People are willing to have sex with inflatable dolls, so initially anything that moves will be an improvement." To some this may all seem like harmless fun, but without any kind of regulation it seems only a matter of time before someone starts selling robotic sex dolls resembling children, says Dr Christensen. This is dangerous ground. Convicted paedophiles might argue that such robots could be used as a form of therapy, while others would object on the grounds that they would only serve to feed an extremely dangerous fantasy.

All of which raises another question. As well as posing physical danger, might robots also be dangerous to humans in less direct ways, by bringing out their worst aspects, from warfare to paedophilia? As Ron Arkin, a roboticist at the Georgia Institute of Technology in Atlanta, puts it: "If you kick a robotic dog, are you then more likely to kick a real one?" Roboticists can do their best to make robots safe—but they cannot reprogram the behaviour of their human masters.

"The question is whether new, robot-specific safety rules and regulations are needed—and, if so, what they should say."

CONTEMPORARY
ISSUES
COMPANION

CHAPTER 2

Emerging AI Technologies

Robotic Cars Are on the Way

Stefanie Olsen

Stefanie Olsen is a staff writer for CNET News. *In the following article she describes coming advances in automotive technology that depend on robotics. A race in the desert sponsored by the Defense Advanced Research Projects Agency (DARPA) has proved that artificially intelligent robots can drive long distances over rugged terrain. Now the developers of those cars are working to apply what has been learned both to future military vehicles and to automobiles. The goal is to make cars safer by using AI to warn drivers, and eventually for automatic obstacle detection and collision avoidance. But robot technology is still a long way from allowing an autonomous machine to handle unpredictable situations.*

A well-publicized race in the desert earlier this month [October 2005] proved that artificially intelligent robots can drive autonomously over rugged terrain and long distances. But will the technology be relevant to average Americans?

If you ask the masterminds behind the robots, the answer is "yes, it's just a matter of time."

Vehicles powered with artificial-intelligence software and sporting the ability to "see" the road with external sensors will be a staple in the U.S. military within 10 years, under a mandate from Congress that spurred the desert robot rally. The underlying technology also will find its way into popular cars with features like collision and lane-departure warnings and adaptive cruise controls. The technology is also relevant, experts say, for the disabled and for automating machines.

"It's not just about a bright idea. There's a lot of work to do. That business of development and productization and building an enterprise is a lot harder than creating a technology," said William "Red" Whittaker, a professor of robotics at Carnegie Mellon University [CMU]. So much robotics research has been done at Carnegie Mellon that CMU's hometown of Pittsburgh is jokingly called "Roboburgh" in some science circles.

Making Cars Safer

For Stanford University, the winner of the DARPA Grand Challenge robot desert race and its $2 million prize, the goal has long been to make vehicles safer for the road.

Stanford set out with the particular interest of developing technology that would help carmakers include aids that could cut down on the number of traffic deaths caused by inattention or intoxication. Now Stanford has $2 million to invest in improving its technology and artificial intelligence research, under the direction of robotics professor Sebastian Thrun. Volkswagen, which sponsored Stanford's vehicle, Stanley, and donated a Touareg V5 for the race, is also developing this technology for its line of cars.

The next frontier will be to develop technologies that can help vehicles improve city driving, as opposed to motoring off-road or on highways, where there are no stoplights or pedestrians. The race gave the robots a structure for driving the course. But on the highway or in cities, intelligent vehicles won't have that direction.

"We've been working on the war on cancer, but with this technology we're a lot closer to saving more lives—young lives—through accidents, by giving attentional aids," said Gary Bradski, a machine-learning expert at Intel who worked on Stanley. "The question is how to alert people without causing an accident."

Four autonomous vehicles—Stanford's Stanley, Carnegie Mellon's H1ghlander and Sandstorm, and Gray Insurance's Kat 5—drove a tricky 132-mile course in the Mojave Desert.

They were the first unmanned cars ever to complete the race designed by DARPA, or the Defense Advanced Research Projects Agency, the research and development arm of the U.S. Department of Defense.

And after only two years of hosting the DARPA Grand Challenge, the U.S. military says it has accomplished its goal of fostering innovation in artificially intelligent designed vehicles. Within 10 years, such vehicles are supposed to make up a third of the U.S. army's transportation.

The technology has already made its way into contractor machinery, and some of the cars showed surprising resilience.

H1ghlander had engine problems the day of the race, which caused it to finish 40 minutes late and ultimately lose the $2 million to Stanford University. Despite its trouble, the car still finished—a testimony to the system software's sturdiness, Carnegie Mellon's Whittaker said. "On its worst day it can run anything," he said.

The same sturdiness is exhibited in robots used by two companies spun out of Whittaker's robotics research. One is RedZone Robotics, which uses robotic machines to make maps of sewer systems. Whittaker also founded Workhorse Technologies, unmanned robots to explore and make maps of mines.

The technology is also being deployed in earth-moving and construction machines from Caterpillar, which was one of the major sponsors of CMU's Red Team.

Future Combat Vehicles

For its future combat system, the government plans to build a family of 18 vehicle types that will be faster and lighter on the road. The group will include so-called drive-by-wire vehicles, as well as some with autonomous and semi-autonomous capabilities. Drive by wire is a car that can be driven without a steering wheel from an internal protected seat or from a remote location, but it is still human operated. The car, perhaps a supply vehicle, could be lightly armored if driven remotely. A semi-autonomous vehicle, on the other hand, can be programmed to travel from point A to point B, or to follow another car.

The autonomous vehicle would be heavily armored and could take GPS (Global Positioning System) coordinates of the road and create a map of obstacles and pass that data back to the semi-autonomous truck. All this could help keep soldiers out of the line of fire.

"There will be programs in the next four or five years, such as tests of semi-autonomous or convoy vehicles in the military," said Bill Klarquist, vice president of engineering at PercepTek, a robotics company that has contracts with the government, Ford and others.

PercepTek creates software for perception planning and control. That's what the car observes about its environment, and given that information, how it will travel. The company develops technology that helps vehicles manage their speed, follow the road and avoid obstacles.

Drive-by-Wire

Carmakers are headed toward total drive-by-wire systems, the route airlines took roughly a decade ago. That means they take the physical actions of the driver, such as pressing on the gas pedal, and turn them into digital messages for the car's central control system. Sensors measure how far the driver turns the steering wheel, for example, and translate that to a message to turn the wheels the appropriate amount. More sophisticated controls can be added for things like emergency braking and traction control.

Many modern cruise control systems already use drive-by-wire throttle functions. With the addition of radar and laser sensors, a car can measure the distance between it and one ahead of it. That way, carmakers can add "adaptive cruise controls" that will regulate the speed of the car to maintain a safe distance between it and other vehicles.

Pricey models from Jaguar, Mercedes and Lexus are already offering that feature.

"Lane keeping" is another benefit of radar and laser sensors. The technology maintains a path down the center of the road and alerts the driver when the car begins to drift into another lane. The feature is already used in the trucking industry, but General Motors has said it plans to offer the feature in cars by 2007.

"The issue is when you introduce new technology there's also the liability. You normally see cars like this introduced in Europe and Japan first, and as they're embraced there, the bugs and characteristics are worked out," Klarquist said.

Adaptive cruise showed up in Germany long before it did in the United States, he said.

In Japan, carmakers have already been testing systems that warn drivers if they're drifting too far out of a lane or if they are about to hit something.

"I think technologically, we're within five to 10 years of having good systems for this," said Intel's Bradski.

Precrash Applications

PercepTek, which backed a robot in the Grand Challenge called Intelligent Design Systems, said that what it will gain from the race is the knowledge of how to use multiple sensors together for road and obstacle detection and avoidance. Commercially, that knowledge will inform what's called precrash applications.

With a combination of laser and radar sensors, a car system could "see" an oncoming collision, if an object ahead was stopping at a faster speed than expected, for example. By detecting how fast the car is traveling in relation to another on the road, the car's system could prepare airbags or cinch seat belts tighter. It could even regulate how the airbags inflate in relation to expected harm from the impact.

John Davidson, whose investment firm Mohr Davidow Ventures sponsored Stanley, predicts that within five years, sophisticated technology for collision avoidance will be in cars.

"Brake systems are already smart, and we'll slowly walk up this curve," Davidson said. "I'm skeptical about ever sitting in the backseat and pressing a button. But the technology has applicability in lots of commercial and industrial applications where autonomy is important."

Machine-learning technology has already touched industries like drug discovery, e-mail processing and financial forecasting. But technology is still a long way from allowing an autonomous machine to handle every unpredicted situation that pops up. "The robot must be able to learn from a situation and think its way through the problem," Davidson said. "But there are other problems they have to solve, like dealing with contingencies. What if a computer dies?"

Robot Working Dogs

Nick D'Alto

Nick D'Alto is an engineer, inventor, and science writer. In the following selection he describes the robot working dogs now being developed. Robot dogs for pets are already common, but now engineers are experimenting with robotic dogs that might be able to do useful jobs such as detecting dangerous toxins or rescuing survivors from fires. Some of these robots have been programmed with "swarm intelligence" that makes them monitor each other's movements, so they exhibit the same kind of pack behavior that real dogs do. Robot dogs for military uses, designed to follow troops into the field and carry supplies over terrain too rough for vehicles, are another possibility, but making them sure-footed is more of a challenge than creating robots that walk on smooth floors.

Welcome to the Robo-Dog Superstore! Model 101 ("Robo-Retriever") is excellent for minding small children. Model 102 is bright and playful. And Model 103 (our cyber-St. Bernard) is an expert at finding lost travelers. Sound like a scene from *The Jetsons*?

Maybe not. After many generations of selection, breeders have succeeded in developing different varieties of real dogs equipped to perform all kinds of useful chores—canines ranging from hard-pulling huskies to super-sniffing bloodhounds. In the hands of expert trainers, real dogs can become eyes and ears for the physically challenged, and learn to do other complex jobs, too.

Now, engineers are working on robot working dogs. OK, they don't have wet noses, and probably won't ever compete with the family pet. But one of them might "sniff out" fallout

Nick D'Alto, "Robo-Dog," *Odyssey*, January 2005, pp. 24–26. Copyright © 2005 Cobblestone Publishing, 30 Grove Street, Suite C, Peterborough, NH 03458. All rights reserved. Reproduced by permission of the publisher.

after a nuclear accident, pull survivors from a raging fire, or perform some other tough job that you wouldn't want to give to a real dog. And since they're designed from the software up, robotic dogs can even help us to better understand the amazing abilities of real dogs.

AI Animals

It all began in 2000, with Sony's AIBO (Artificial Intelligence Robot), the first mass-marketed robotic dog. This programmable pooch is a machine capable of playing and learning just like a real pet . . . well, in some ways. Maybe you've seen one. As it turns out, though, in terms of evolution AIBO was simply a robo-puppy. Since then, inventors from military designers to college students have been "breeding" a bold new generation of cyber-mutts.

Of course, in the world of robotic dogs, the breeders are computer hackers. So at Yale University's Feral Dog Robotics Program (http://xdesign.eng.yale.edu/feralrobots), engineering students begin by dismantling off-the-shelf robot dogs (such as AIBO, Megabyte, and Jimmy Neutron's dog, Goddard). Then, they upgrade these toy dogs with off-the-wall electronics.

The result? Some remarkable new cyber-pooches. New "brains" (microprocessors) make these dogs smarter. Then, a new "nose" (a toxin sensor) lets them "sniff out" environmental poisons. For roaming over rough terrain, better mechanical linkages make them stronger and faster.

Not Your Typical Yale Bulldogs

It's all the brainchild of Dr. Natalie Jeremijenko, Yale University engineering instructor and self-described techno-artist (she studies how people interact with machines).

Let loose in a field polluted years before by industrial runoff, her students' robot dogs even exhibit the same pack behavior that real dogs use to hunt more effectively. How? While genetics gives real dogs these social behaviors, the robots have been programmed with "swarm intelligence," logic that makes them monitor each other's movements and then follow the dog with the strongest sensor readings.

Just as bloodhounds and other bomb-sniffing dogs can be trained to recognize characteristic scents, the Yale robots detect concentrations of VOCs (volatile organic compounds) and other dangerous toxins. They are perfect for evaluating the safety of parks, school yards, and other public spaces. Cameras (mounted on the dogs' rumps!) allow researchers to observe their interaction with handlers as they scurry about the field.

Dogged Research

The robo trend is spreading. Russian roboteers plan to sic their own souped-up toy dogs on fallout sites from the Chernobyl nuclear disaster. Australian robo-dingos may be sent to fetch lingering evidence of early atomic tests Down Under.

Tough work for a toy? "There's an army of these innocent-looking playthings out there," the Feral Dog Web site advises. "But watch out! These are really semiautonomous robotic creatures—just waiting for further instructions!"

Speak, Boy, Speak!

Real dogs are language masters. In fact, German researchers have reported that a border collie named Rico can understand a vocabulary of over 200 words—just like a 2-year-old child. But do dogs acquire language the same way children do?

At Sony Artificial Intelligence Research in Paris, Professor Luc Steels is using a robot dog to find out. By adding a state-of-the-art speech recognition system to an AIBO dog, his team is gaining insight into how children (and dogs) learn to associate objects with words.

Their verdict? "You cannot just show the robot an object and say, 'Ball,'" observes the professor. "You need to encourage and correct. Robots, dogs, and toddlers all learn through social interaction."

Run, Spot, Run!

At Boston Dynamics Corporation, engineers are gaining similar appreciation for the way dogs run. Their motivation? A multimillion-dollar program by the U.S. Army's Tank-automotive and Armaments Command (or TACOM) to build a new kind of Rin-Tin-Tin (with an emphasis on the "tin"!). It's a mechanical dog designed to follow military troops into the field. This fleet-footed cyber-hound would carry supplies (the way huskies do) over terrain too rough for wheeled vehicles, or even storm up flights of stairs to raid a terrorist lair.

Yet, while the present generation of robots is perfectly capable of walking across smooth floors, duplicating the sure-footed gait of a real hunting dog is quite a challenge. Real dogs use a complex feedback process to correct and maintain their balance. They also use an intuitive process to recognize and avoid obstacles. Scientists at NASA's Jet Propulsion Laboratory (Pasadena, CA) are working on multiple camera "eyes" to give robotic dogs the basics of depth perception.

Well Wirth It

If building robotic dogs sounds like a race, then engineer Nick Wirth, a designer of Formula One race cars, may have an edge. His latest pooch, a PC on legs, can walk, climb, and even read e-mails with a synthesized voice. Its cameras and microphones detect movement—just as a guard dog does. And like the cartoon mutt "Marmaduke," this big cyber-pooch is strong enough (thanks to a carbon-fiber frame) to lift a 5-year-old child.

So, will tomorrow's robotic canine serve as a Seeing Eye dog for the blind, using robotic vision? Or help a patient with multiple sclerosis, via electromechanical muscles? Or serve in the military? Or do other things we haven't even thought of yet?

Like their real ancestors domesticated ages ago, specialized cyberhounds may one day enter into new, mutually beneficial, social relationships with us, too. From all appearances, whenever science calls, new "breeds" of robotic dogs will increasingly be ready to "Come!"

Building Intelligent Machines by Copying Living Brains

Douglas Fox

Douglas Fox is a science writer who lives in California. In the following article he explains the new approach to artificial intelligence (AI) that is being used by scientists who are designing robot brains by imitating real brains. In the past, AI was based on mere computer models of what a living brain does, and there is still a great deal that is not known about how brains work which cannot be discovered through such modeling. Now, researchers are creating robots with neural connections like those in animal brains and are recording the changes in these hundreds of thousands of connections while these robots explore and learn. They hope that eventually, robots designed in this way will be able to learn much more than computers can learn. It has been found that having a body is crucial to brain development. Some scientists believe all AI research should be done with robots that have bodies and can move as they learn, while others think more progress can be made by starting with mathematical processes that are well understood.

The infant crawls across a floor strewn with blocks, grabbing and tasting as it goes, its malleable mind impressionable and hungry to learn. Before my eyes it is already adapting, discovering that the striped blocks are yummy and the spotted ones taste bad.

Its exploration is driven by instincts: an interest in bright objects, a predilection for tasting things, and an innate notion of what tastes good. This, after all, is how babies explore the world and discover that pink, perky objects exist, and that they produce milk. Hands-on exploration moulds their billions of untrained brain cells into a fully functioning brain.

The infant I am watching wander around its rather spartan playpen in the Neurosciences Institute (NSI) in La Jolla, California, is a more limited creature. It is a trashcan-shaped robot called Darwin VII, and it has just 20,000 brain cells. Despite this, it has managed to master the abilities of an 18-month-old baby—a pretty impressive feat for a machine.

The key to Darwin's abilities is its brain. This is an amalgam of rat and ape brains, encoded in a computer program that controls its actions. Darwin tastes blocks by grabbing them with its metal jaws to see if they produce electricity. It likes the ones that do and dislikes the ones that don't. Within half an hour of being switched on it learned to find the tasty blocks.

Darwin VII is the fourth in a series of robots that Jeff Krichmar and his colleagues at NSI have created in a quest to better understand how our own brains work—the first three versions of Darwin did not have a real robotic body to control. Darwin VII allows Krichmar to record changes in hundreds of thousands of its brain's neural connections as it explores and learns, to test neuroscientists' theories of how real brains work. "This is something that you can't do in a real brain," Krichmar points out.

A New Approach to AI

If Krichmar and others like him succeed, robots like Darwin might one day be seen as the ancestors of something much bigger. Some researchers, and even the US Defense Advanced Research Projects Agency, are gambling that robots like Darwin will be the forebears of an entirely new approach to artificial intelligence (AI): building intelligent machines by copying the structures of living brains. Some groups are even designing microchips that could eventually be used to build anatomically realistic artificial silicon brains to replace the computers that power existing robots like Darwin.

The dream is that these new brains, embedded in robotic bodies of silicon and steel, will go to a level beyond today's artificial intelligence systems. By sensing their environments as they explore and learn, they will develop the ability to survive in the constantly changing real world of imperfect information that we navigate so effortlessly, but which computers have yet to master. They will learn to do anything from mundane household chores we'd rather not do, to driving the kids to school, and even autonomously explore Mars or run nuclear waste facilities, all without human intervention. "All you would have to do is teach them," says Juyang Weng, a developmental roboticist at Michigan State University in East Lansing.

These systems will arise, say the researchers, by emulating the brain's neurons and the way they are connected to each other. In animal brains neurons are linked to form huge reconfigurable networks that behave like filters, transferring, modifying or blocking signals that they receive. Though living brains have been studied for decades, we still don't know exactly how they achieve the amazing abilities of the human mind.

That hasn't stopped computer scientists from trying to imitate them. The idea of an artificial neural network that could perform computations was proposed as long ago as 1943, by Warren McCullough and Walter Pitts at the University of Illinois. In the decades since, efforts to create intelligent machines from these networks progressed in relative isolation from the study of how real brains work. As a result, these artificial neural networks bear little relation to the structure of neural networks in real brains. But in the past few years, neuroscientists and AI researchers have started collaborating more closely, and their labours are beginning to bear fruit. Their conclusions challenge two decades of research into artificial neural networks.

It all boils down to this: existing artificial neural networks, such as those used in many computer systems today, are totally inadequate for creating anything resembling animal, let alone human, intelligence. To do that, you have to be as faithful as possible to the real thing. And for the first time that's what several groups around the world are trying to do: emulate both the structure and the function of living brains in detail.

Structure and Function Are Linked

In all neural networks, both artificial and real, structure and function are intimately linked. The pattern of connections between neurons determines how well the network performs a particular task. If you train an artificial neural network to recognise abnormal cells in smear tests, for example, it adapts by adjusting connections between individual neurons until external feedback indicates to the network it is doing the job well. But unlike the human brain, these systems are optimised to perform a single task. "It is a small part of what might be happening in the brain, a tiny portion of an intelligent action," says Igor Aleksander of Imperial College London.

To get the adaptive, flexible behaviour you see in animals, you need to imitate the design of a whole brain, the body it lives in and the drives that motivate it, Krichmar says. "A brain-based device provides them all; a traditional neural net simply doesn't."

Neuroscientists have identified hundreds of different neural areas within mammalian brains. In effect each is a specialised neural network unto itself. It is only when you recreate these areas and start interconnecting the different modules that complex behaviour emerges that no single part of the system could achieve on its own, Aleksander says.

Back in Krichmar's lab, I watch as Darwin VII approaches another block. On a computer screen in front of me a map of its brain lights up. Groups of its simulated neurons that recognise patterns light up to identify the stripes on the block. Darwin has 18 simulated neural areas, including a lower visual area that detects edges and a motor area that directs movement. Its brain even simulates a virtual squirt of the pleasure-inducing neurotransmitter dopamine whenever it tastes a yummy block. This positive reinforcement encourages Darwin to repeat actions that lead to it finding those tasty blocks in the first place. I watch the result of that trained response as Darwin recognises a striped block. The mere sight of a block causes Darwin's motor area to light up in anticipation, triggering a reflex response. It lunges forward to grab it.

It's a neat demonstration, but since Darwin's brain is buried in a computer simulation, I wonder how much it really does resemble a real brain. To show me, Krichmar pulls up a computer file describing Darwin's brain. "We choose these values based on what we know of animal neurons in these brain areas," he says. These numbers represent a model of a brain based on the neural activity measured in laboratory experiments on rat and ape brains. It describes the topology and types of connection between individual neurons and the neural regions of Darwin's brain.

Robot Brains Based on Real Ones

While the structure of traditional artificial neural networks bears little resemblance to living brains, the details of Darwin's brain are grounded in reality, Krichmar says. He and his colleagues laboriously assembled these details by scouring published research. From this they extracted a wide range of data, including functional MRI scans of brains showing points of activity in response to different sights or smells, and neural connections mapped by painstakingly injecting single nerve cells with dye and then, by microscope, tracing the cell's hundreds of branches that lit up. . . .

Using his most sophisticated robot to date, Darwin X, Krichmar has been studying how brains use landmarks to navigate. Starting from different points in a room each time, the robot's task was to find a hidden floor marker, using stripes painted on the walls as landmarks. As the robot learned the layout of the room, it developed "place neurons" in its virtual hippocampus that helped it home in on the marker three times as fast on the 10th attempt as it did on the first. The place cells had not been implicitly encoded Krichmar says. "They just emerged from the model." He says the same thing can be seen in the hippocampal cells of a rat.

Weng has seen similar results with a robot named SAIL (Self-Organising Autonomous Incremental Learner). It operates in a slightly different way to the Darwin robots, focusing less on copying brain anatomy and more on mimicking how connections between individual neurons organise themselves as a brain matures.

When SAIL is switched on for the first time, Weng takes it for a stroll, leading it through the corridors of the building. After a day of this kind of guided activity, he lets SAIL navigate under looser supervision. If the robot hits a wall it gets negative feedback signals from bumper sensors, if it gets to the end of the corridor without hitting a wall, Weng presses a button on the robot that "rewards" it. . . .

Not All in the Mind

Having a physical body is another crucial element steering the development of Darwin's and SAIL's brains, just as it does for living ones. In 1963, Richard Held and Alan Hein at Brandeis University, Massachusetts, published a report on an experiment that showed how crucial this is in living brains. They raised 10 pairs of kittens so their only exposure to light came when they were attached to a circular, rotating table top, like a lazy Susan. One kitten always rode enclosed in a box on the edge of the table. It could see but not walk. The other kitten was attached to the opposite side of the table by a harness, so it could walk in circles, rotating the table top and the first kitten with it. Both kittens saw the same view of the room as they turned, but one's visual experience was caused by its own activity, whereas the other's was not. This small difference had a huge impact. The kitten that pulled the turntable round developed normal depth perception within a few days; the kitten that merely rode on it did not.

The kittens developed such different responses because of the way the nervous system is wired. As a kitten steps forward, the nerves driving that movement notify the brain of that step, so it can adjust its interpretation of visual information. Disembodied artificial neural networks trapped in a desktop computer can't experience this. But being mobile, Darwin and SAIL do. They use movement to enhance what they learn from what they see. Darwin VII learns to recognise striped blocks by moving, so that it sees them from countless perspectives. SAIL uses movement to distinguish door frames from posters and other vertical edges. "You really do need a body," says roboticist Oliver Brock at the University of Massachusetts, Amherst.

Most AI robots of the past two decades used elaborate modelling systems to describe the real world around them, but failed on simple common-sense tasks. To make them function, programmers had to tackle the monumental task of anticipating all the likely objects in a robot's environment and how they might change. Will AI robots that combine movement with a brain-like neural network fare better? "I give a resounding yes to that," says Aleksander, who sees this approach as a way out of the hole into which traditional AI has dug itself.

Even SAIL, which starts each task with completely blank neurons, was able to overcome problems that seriously taxed other AI systems. First its brain developed areas to represent straight edges, then it combined these into relevant categories such as doorways and cabinets. And it did all this without a programmer's guidance.

Does that mean all other efforts to develop AI should be dropped in favour of developing systems that combine robot-like movement and neural-style processing? Stephen Muggle-ton, a computer scientist at Imperial College London, isn't convinced. "You may make more rapid progress by starting from well-defined mathematical processes," he says. These can be inspired by the brain, but they shouldn't be copied from it.

But [Anil] [a theoretical neuroscientist at NSI] insists that in an unpredictable world, mimicking the brain on a detailed level will provide advantages that other approaches cannot. For example, real brains often have a lot of redundancy when it comes to performing a particular task. Similar redundancy might allow a brain-based robot to continue to function even if part of its brain is damaged.

Slowly Darwin and his friends are leaving their playpens and heading out into the real world. The latest version in the Darwin series is learning to play soccer riding on a Segway.

Could such a robot one day even become conscious? Seth and Krichmar are both convinced it's possible. "I don't see any reason why it couldn't happen," says Krichmar. But as I watch Darwin VII pootle around the lab, it's clear that having a brain is only half the problem. Would you entrust your child's life, or the safety of nuclear waste disposal site to a clumsy if intelligent trashcan?

The Impact of Robots on Employment

Arnold Brown

Arnold Brown is chairman of the board of the World Future Society. In the following viewpoint he considers changes in the relationship between people and machines that may occur with advances in robotics. Already, intelligent computer software and robots are taking on many jobs formerly done by people. This trend will increase in the near future, even apart from the possibility that humanoid robots might someday become slaves of humans and demand rights. In Brown's opinion, it is likely that progress in robotics may lead to a technophobic movement when displaced human workers, including professionals and managers, become angry and afraid. Furthermore, as mechanical and computerized creations perform more and more tasks, society may need to redefine what it means to be human.

A world run by robots is no longer a notion exclusive to science fiction. The first glimmers of the coming robotic era are already visible.

There are now more than 1.5 million robot vacuum cleaners in use. Robot rovers explore the surface of Mars. Microsoft has created robot teddy bears capable of monitoring kids. Another Microsoft robot, SmartPhlow, will monitor and control traffic flows. There are now even robot camel jockeys in the Middle East.

Signs of the growing prevalence of robotic technology are all around us. But we have yet to fully explore the consequences of our increasing dependence on these machines and the numerous ways they are inserting themselves into our daily lives.

Arnold Brown, "The Robotic Economy: Brave New World or a Return to Slavery?" *Futurist*, July–August 2006, pp. 50–55. © 2006 World Future Society. All rights reserved. Reproduced by permission of The World Future Society.

The mechanical slaves of the twenty-first century will perform tasks deemed too hazardous for humans, such as cleaning up toxic waste. Others, deliberately made to resemble humans, will be companions and teachers of children. Some will even be chimeras made up partly of human cells. And, increasingly, they will be both self-repairing and self-reproducing.

If you discard the word "robot," which was coined by Karl [Karel] Čapek in the play *R.U.R.*, you might find that the most apt term for the machines that will increasingly do our manual labor, operate and direct interactions between people and institutions, perform domestic services, fight our wars, take care of children and seniors, clean up our messes, and so on may be *slaves*.

Robots are not free. They are owned. As of now, they enjoy none of the rights we associate with free human beings. At the same time, our economic prosperity (and much else) is dependent not only on the competency of these increasingly intelligent devices and systems, but also on their compliance.

Japan Leads the Way

Much of the impetus for robot development comes from Japan, where demographic trends and labor costs are creating a growing market for machines that can replace humans. Hitachi's robot EMIEW can be trained to do any number of factory and office jobs. Virtual pets, such as Neapets, are astoundingly popular in Japan, and their popularity is spreading. One robot toy—Pleo, a dinosaur—is designed to elicit emotional responses from children and adjust its own behavior in turn. A group of Japanese scientists has invented a soccer-playing robot called VisiON; they claim a team of such robots will win the World Cup by 2050. Japanese engineers are rushing to produce humanoid robots to care for the aged as well as children. Also in development are robots that can monitor and assist the elderly in taking medications and help blind people navigate and shop in grocery stores.

The South Korean government intends to roboticize that country, based on a vision of a robot-centered intelligent society.

The U.S. military is another major supporter of robotics. The Pentagon is developing managed "trauma pods" to perform battlefield surgery and plans to spend more than $120 billion to develop what will eventually become autonomous robot soldiers.

As these machines become more humanoid—in appearance, in personality, in thinking—how will their relationship to humans develop? The proliferation of these robots will surely generate much controversy as society ponders what such machines might be legally entitled to. One can imagine a fair amount of resistance to the notion of extending robots (or semi-human robots) the same rights afforded to people, such as the right to own property, vote, or run for office. But discrimination against bionic or semi-bionic entities may be difficult to defend on legal grounds, especially as growing numbers of humans incorporate machinery into their biological functioning.

"Othersourcing" Human Jobs

Much of the sound and fury in U.S. politics in the 2004 election arose from the volatile issues of *outsourcing*—the movement of work to other entities and other places. The most contentious part of that issue was offshoring, which refers to moving work and jobs to other countries. This particular issue is now creating concern in Europe, as well.

As the effort to break down work processes into components progresses, more and more knowledge work can be outsourced to countries with a lower living wage than places like the United States. As is usual with political sound and fury, the real underlying issue has been obscured by all the noise.

That real issue is *othersourcing*—the increasing ability to have work done not only off-site and by other entities (such as unanticipated competitors) but by nonhumans.

"Over the next 10 years, the rate of IT [information technology] job loss that can be attributed to automation will be about double what we think will be due to outsourcing," says Neil MacDonald, analyst of the research and advisory company Gartner.

The firm or organization as we have always known it has been a job-creating mechanism. Even when machines have displaced people, the effect has been temporary, because the ultimate outcome of technology has been more jobs. But as work has become more abstract and impersonal—as we have gone from making and growing things to marketing and servicing them—it has become easier to depersonalize work and to see workers as abstract, too.

This trend, together with the extraordinary technological advances of recent years, is leading to a potentially massive shift of increasingly higher kinds of work to machines and software. It has also become easier for unexpected competitors to create a cost or efficiency advantage that can gain them all or part of a business function. This othersourcing shift is seen not only in every kind of business, but also in government, military, and nonprofit activities:

- Computer software models direct the allocation of pharmaceutical company representatives' time and determine the prioritization of customers.

- In many business operations, there is so much information that only computer programs, cellular automata, can process it.

- In many areas of science, experts believe that, because of the overwhelming volume of data, only robot scientists will be able to process it.

- Automated software can cut gemstones as well as or better than humans.

- In the future, airplanes will communicate directly with each other, eliminating the need for human air traffic controllers.

- NASA is developing nanobots for "autonomous nano-technology swarms" that will know when and how to form shapes and patterns for planetary exploration.

- Robots are being taught to work as teams, using common intelligence.

According to the Robotics Industries Association, sales of factory robots increased 28% in 2005, which comes on top of a 20% rise in 2004. By some estimates, the international market for robotic manufacturing units is already $5 billion.

From Humankind to Mindkind

In the world of employment, resources have already begun to shift thanks not so much to robotics as to better communications technology. Business leaders have begun to see a growing distinction between right-brain skills and left-brain skills, and they are finding new ways to procure and leverage each. Othersourcing is now extending to many more white-collar jobs where the brain-work is becoming, or has already become, commoditized—even in the field of medicine and drugs. For example, you can buy software to do your taxes instead of having to go to an accountant. This knowledge commoditization will be exacerbated as higher education and technical capabilities expand in lesser developed, lower-wage countries.

Creative work may seem like precisely the sort of area where human workers will remain dominant. But technology is affecting jobs here as well. Instead of hiring whole *people* to do creative work, managers at many firms are shifting to hiring *minds*—which don't necessarily have to be human. Eli Lilly's e-business venture, InnoCentive, has more than 85,000 registered "solvers" from 173 countries. Corporations post their biology and chemistry needs on the InnoCentive Web site, hoping that one of the registered researchers will be able to provide a solution.

Similarly, office supply giant Staples held a competition and received 8,300 submissions from customers who came up with new product ideas. Automaker BMW accessed customer creativity by allowing people to post on the company Web site their suggestions for ways to leverage advance telematics and in-car online services. Meanwhile, the BBC has announced its "Creative Archive License," providing public access to its full media archives so that individuals can participate in the production of entertainment.

Initiatives such as these reduce the need for bricks and mortar to house bodies, and all the overhead that comes with hiring people, while expanding the universe of potentially harnessable minds, whatever form they come in. Along with this, the focus will begin to shift away from managing people and toward project management—putting together all the varied resources and components, wherever available and in whatever form, to accomplish the desired task or vision. As organizational energy input continues to migrate away from labor, and organizations that do depend on labor seek out the lowest-cost providers, the management of labor will be less important and the processing and management of information will take center stage.

At some point, even human minds may be superfluous. IBM, École Polytechnique de Lausanne, and others are working toward computer models of the human brain—the key step in designing a computer that will "think" on a par with humans. [Computer scientist and entrepreneur] Ray Kurzweil predicts that we will have an artificial brain that can recognize patterns as human brains do by 2020. But we can already see signs of that distant possibility today. IBM consulting uses a software program that chooses and allocates resources for projects better and faster than humans can. Cisco is using software programs to replace humans in human resources, finance, customer service, and other staff areas.

Another major factor fueling these developments is the increasing complexity of the information age. Recent research shows that people cannot efficiently handle complex problems—those with more than four variables—so we will come more and more to rely on machines to do not only what we don't want to do, but also what we can't do.

Working with Robotic Slaves

Questions are already being raised in literature, film, and TV shows about the present and future relationship between humans and these new slaves. Years ago the movie *Spartacus* showed the causes and consequences of revolt by human slaves in ancient Rome. Recent movies such as *Blade Runner; I, Robot*; and *Terminator* depict similar—and in many ways more frightening—revolts by nonhuman slaves.

Many economies in the past were slave-based. In ancient Greece, such an economy gave rise to an extraordinarily creative society. In other societies, results were less beneficial. In the twenty-first century, a new slave-based economy is developing, and we have to wonder what the consequences of that will be.

Slave owning can have a corrupting effect, and in some ways it can rob both an economy and a society of energy and aspiration. Furthermore, machines, like humans, can be corrupted. Certainly, the persistent and exasperating problems of software serve as a constant reminder of that corruptibility, as does the common excuse from your banker—"the computer is down." It is estimated that at least 1 million infected computers around the world have been formed into "bot nets," controlled from outside and used to steal identities and surreptitiously install spyware or adware. Advances in technology seem always to bring on problems of control. As transistors get smaller, for example, they become less reliable and predictable, as will the robots and other machines containing them.

The idea of human slavery has not disappeared. One recent report says that at least 12.3 million people in the world are in forced labor—bondage. Others report that the number may exceed 25 million, most of whom are in the sex trade or domestic service.

The machines that we're accustomed to—dishwashers, washing machines, alarm clocks, automatic transmissions, etc.—are clearly inanimate objects. But as more of the machines we own are endowed with human qualities, whether in their appearance or in a nascent ability to think, how will we see the relationship? How will they?

Relations Between People and Machines

For managers of organizations, these are not just idle questions. The relationships in the workplace between people and machines, already somewhat difficult, will become more complex and uncertain. Managers will have to think increasingly of how to get a specific task done rather than who will do it. Human-resource [HR] management is developing into human-machine interface management. HR personnel will need new and different training and experience to do their jobs effectively. Customer relations and service will also be entering new ground. As more of the contact between customers goes through machines, we will require a better understanding of the psychology of such relationships and the effects on customer attitudes and behaviors. (Two institutions that have proven to be leaders in this research area are the MIT [Massachusetts Institute of Technology] Media Lab and the Human-Computer Interaction Lab at Wichita State University.)

As a result of the coming advances in robotics, it is likely that we will see a renewed Luddite movement. This second technophobic movement could well be more difficult to deal with than the one involving machine smashers of the nineteenth century. Employers will be under pressure, from within as well as from politicians and the media, to help those whose jobs will be lost. Retraining programs could help ease the pressure and will most likely be seen as good community relations.

One solution, which could supplement unemployment insurance, is trade adjustment insurance. Meanwhile, as staff and management functions become mechanized, employers will need to explore in depth what the consequences will be as more professionals and managers become afraid and angry. Already facing high costs and inconvenience from theft and sabotage, employers should have a comprehensive other-sourcing strategy that anticipates the problems that naturally occur with high layoffs. Businesses could form cooperative skill banks so that employees whose particular skills have been rendered redundant by other-sourcing could be made available to other companies that still need them.

The robotic era may also force us to rethink our tendency to measure people's value solely in terms of their economic contributions. Robotics pioneer Hans Moravec has speculated that, by the year 2050, entire corporations will exist with no human employees, or investors, at all. Yet, there still exists a role for humans in the future workplace. Imagination, empathy, and compassion are still the exclusive domain of *Homo sapiens*, and, in our automated future, business managers should seize the opportunity to rediscover and encourage these traits in their workers as well as in their customers and users.

The bigger challenge may be learning to live with our progeny even as they surpass us in intelligence and capability. As our mechanical and computerized creations perform more of the tasks formerly performed by humans, and as they come to resemble us to a greater degree, we may need to reconsider more than simply how we interact with these devices. We may need to entirely redefine what it means to be human.

Robots for Fighting Future Wars

Milan Vesely

Milan Vesely is a Kenya-born journalist who lives in the United States. In the following article he describes the U.S. military's hopes to use robots in combat. On the one hand, this might save the lives of many human soldiers, but on the other hand, computer-savvy young insurgents might hack into the robots' programming and turn them against their original masters. So it is not yet known how effective they would be. Intelligent machines mounted on tracks are already being used for bomb disposal. Nevertheless, even advocates of robotic soldiers are not sure they can ever replace fighting men. Moreover, trusting robots with life-or-death decisions would surely raise ethical issues and questions of responsibility. Yet the monetary and political cost of sending human soldiers into battle is so high that robots may be rushed into the field before their usefulness has been proven.

The scene is familiar, the Internet video tape grainy and slightly out of focus. A long line of US military vehicles is racing along the Baghdad airport road when suddenly one is enveloped in flames, the blast scatters pieces of palm tree and metal in a deadly 100-yard arc. Then comes the gunfire, rocket-propelled grenades flying in. Soon another sound joins in, as the Medevac helicopters arrive.

But that scene may lack one important ingredient in the future. The helicopter may not be a Medevac one, its medical personnel replaced by eyeglass-wearing computer geeks with handheld laptops rapidly punching keyboards to get the truck back up and running.

Milan Vesely, "The Robot Revolution," *Middle East*, April 2005, pp. 22–25. Copyright 2005 IC Publications Ltd. Reproduced by permission.

Welcome to the 21st Century US soldier; programmed robots that can do anything from drive an ammunition truck guided by global positioning system (GPS) coordinates to firing a 1,000-rounds-a-minute M60 machine gun to beat off attacking insurgents.

American military planners predict such robots will in the future become the major fighting force in wars such as that currently being fought in Iraq. "They don't get hungry, they're not afraid, they don't forget their orders, and they don't care if the robot next to them gets shot," Gordon Johnson of the Joint Forces Command at Pentagon headquarters says, his confidence based on the results of field trials now underway.

But will they do a better job than the humans they replace, or will technically minded insurgents hack into the command codes and redirect the robot's lethality back against their original masters?—that is still an open question for military analysts.

Robo-Soldiers May Reduce Death Toll

The IED (Improvised Explosive Device) has proved the insurgent's most effective weapon in the Iraqi conflict. Crude but safe for the attacker hidden 100 yards away in the palm grove, and highly lethal, the IED has developed from a stand-off weapon detonated by wires, to a weapon ignited by a cellphone or wireless line-of-sight computer signal.

The damage these devices have inflicted on the US military is vast, [as of early 2005] some 1,600 soldiers killed and at least 12,000 wounded since the Iraqi conflict began. But now with robo-soldiers rapidly being brought into the arena the toll is expected to drop dramatically, and a whole new era of warfare is about to begin.

The robotic soldier has been a Pentagon dream for 30 years. To achieve this, Pentagon planners have backed it to the hilt financially, allocating some $127bn [billion] to a project called Future Combat Systems, or FCS. . . .

The projected increase in funding for robot-soldiers is based on two assumptions; one already proven, one tantalisingly in sight. Following the success of track-mounted robots in Afghanistan where they have been successfully used to clear caves of booby traps and ambushes, US military planners believe that robot soldiers that think, see, and react increasingly like humans are possible. Advances in nanotechnology—the science of miniaturisation—make this goal achievable, they argue; crude examples are already able to mimic the walking gait of a normal human being.

Battle-ready robots able to transport ammunition, gather intelligence and/or search and blow up buildings are already being tested, the first such thinking machine mounted on miniature tracks is expected to arrive in Iraq [in April 2005].

With a 1,000-round-a-minute M60 machine gun mounted on a 360-degree swivel, this bomb disposal machine will take up frontline positions, its machine gun able to deal death to any sighted enemy within a 1,000 yard radius. Already used to dig up roadside bombs, this latest version of robo-soldier will be a radio controlled fighter, its computerised memory allowing it to react automatically to incoming fire.

"It's more than just a dream now," Johnson of the robotics effort at the Joint Forces Command Research Centre, says. "Today we have an infantry soldier. We give him a set of instructions; if you find the enemy, this is what you do. We give the soldier enough information to recognise the enemy when he is fired upon. He is autonomous but he has to operate under certain controls. By 2015 we think we can do the same infantry missions with robots. The American military will certainly have these kinds of robots," Johnson asserts firmly. "It's not a question of if; it's just a question of when."

Robots May Not Replace Men

Many of the robo-soldier's advocates are not so sure that machines can ever replace the fighting human being however.

"War will always be a human endeavour, one with death and disaster ever present," Robert Finkelstein, president of Robotic Technology in Potomac, Maryland, says. "It could take up to 2030 to develop a robot that looks, thinks, and fights like a soldier. The Pentagon's goal is there, but the path is not totally clear yet."

And what of the insurgents; how will America's enemies counter a machine capable of spewing death while at the same time being protected by the latest advances in armour-plating? Will they turn its capabilities to their own advantage, much as they have countered the jamming signals used to disable their IED's in Iraq?

"Will they decipher the operating codes; turn a robot's lethality back onto the operators via electronic hacking, or even capture a robot and re-programme it to recognise the US military as the enemy?" some computer experts wonder. One thing US military observers are certain about; it won't be long before counter-robot techniques surface and possibly even crude counter-robots appear to take on the real thing on the battlefield.

"After all, a child's radio-controlled toy vehicle filled with explosives could disable the robo-soldier if it explodes close by," one military expert says. "Such items are now commonly sold at toy stores, the larger ones capable of carrying up to 10 pounds of high explosives."

As has been seen in Iraq, technology is not the preserve of the US military alone. Each gruesome killing or deadly attack by the insurgents is shown on the Internet within minutes. The world is able to view the terrorist's actions even before any official announcement or CNN report is broadcast.

Computer savvy, the younger insurgents are certain to take the arrival of the new soldiers as a personal challenge, certain to test their skills against the computer and wireless guided robo-soldier, much as they have against the radio jamming devices now used to protect US convoys on Iraqi highways.

Questions over the Geneva Convention and its rules of conduct during warfare undertaken by robo-soldiers are now being raised. As history shows, every breakthrough in military technology leaves the ethical laws scrambling to catch up, the arrival of the longbow, the tank and the atomic bomb being some more obvious examples.

Can Robots Be Trusted to Make Decisions?

Trusting robots with life and death decisions at a roadblock is sure to raise issues and questions of responsibility, especially in the event of so called "friendly fire".

"The lawyers tell me there are no prohibitions against robots making life or death decisions," Johnson says. "I have even been asked what happens if the robot destroys a school bus rather then a nearby tank." In a statement sure to be challenged by human rights activists Johnson states: "We will not entrust a robot with that decision until we are confident they can make it."

Others, like Bill Joy—a co-founder of Sun Microsystems—are not so sure that the trend to robots making their own decisions is all that smart. Writing in *Wired* magazine, Joy says: "As machines become more intelligent people will let them make more of their decisions for them. A stage may be reached at which the decisions necessary to keep the system running will be so complex humans will be incapable of making them intelligently. At that stage of development the machines themselves will be in effective control."

Not surprisingly, money is a major factor in the US military's decision to mechanise its fighting forces. Future commitments for soldiers' retirement benefits already total $653bn [billion], a figure the military is unable to come up with if called upon to do so. The current median cost per basic infantry man is $4m [thousand] and growing, the cost of maintaining, or scrapping, a worn-out robot estimated at a tenth of that figure. To have robots do at least the basic tasks therefore makes economic sense to a US military watching the mounting cost of modern armaments with increasing alarm.

To design a human replica is one of the most daunting aspects of the new technology. A four-foot high prototype with a single cyclops eye and a gun for a right arm is already being tested. In laboratory conditions this robot can aim and fire at a tin can, the first such machine able to identify targets and shoot at them. "We're at the mammal stage of development now," Jeff Grossman of the Space and Naval Warfare Systems Centre in San Diego says. "We're trying to get to the level of a primate where we are making sensible decisions."

Five categories of robots are envisioned by the US military. In addition to the hunter/killer cyclops prototype mentioned above, one robot is designed to scout buildings, tunnels and caves, a third will haul ammunition, weapons and gear as well as perform basic intelligence gathering, a fourth will be a drone in flight and a fifth originally designed for guard duty will be able to conduct psychological warfare and other missions. Most successful has been a robot driver, its progress far enough along so that operational models are already being tested at the Army Research Laboratory's Aberdeen Proving Grounds in Maryland. . . .

As the insurgency in Iraq continues to grind away, the American military is bound to rush robots into the field before their capability has been fully proven. "The cost of the soldier in the field is so high, both in cash and in the political sense, that robots will be doing wildly dangerous tasks in battle in the very near future," says Colin M. Angle, 37, co-founder and chief executive of iRobot. How soon their human opponents will figure out a way of negating or even turning their advantages back on to their handlers will be an interesting issue, the time lag not too distant if the current conflict is any indicator. In that case, grainy, out-of-focus videos of two sets of robots duelling it out in a Fallujah street may not be that far away.

CHAPTER 3

I Humanoid Robots

Should Robots Look Just Like Humans?

Daniel Harris

Daniel Harris is the digital technology editor for Electronic Design *magazine. In the following article he reports that researchers disagree about how humanlike robots should be. Japanese scientists aim to make them look as much like humans as possible because Japanese people, especially children and the elderly, are very accepting of robots. In the West, however, people look upon robots as machines to make their lives better and do not want to forget that they are machines. For this reason, although Honda's Advanced Step in Innovative Mobility (ASIMO) robot has human shape so that it can operate efficiently in caring for the elderly and disabled, it was deliberately designed to look artificial. Researchers at Osaka University in Japan, in contrast, are trying to create androids with bodies that appear indistinguishable from humans.*

Soon, robots will be able to help the elderly and disabled answer the door, prepare a meal, take their medicine, and even get from a bed to a wheelchair. As the number of retirees in the U.S., Japan, and other parts of the world continues to rise at an alarming rate, the need for robotic assistants becomes more prevalent.

A number of factors play into this need. More and more people are waiting until later in life to have children, making it difficult for adult children to care for elderly parents. And with the rising cost of healthcare, it's becoming increasingly costly for patients and their families to afford home health aides, personal nurses, and the like. So if robots can become affordable (and insurance companies would be willing to contribute to the cost), the non-human caregivers could revolutionize the way healthcare is provided.

The changing face of healthcare is prompting companies like Honda to kick their research into high gear. Yet researchers disagree about how these robots should appear and operate.

Two Researchers, Two Opinions

Hiroshi Ishiguro, a professor in Osaka University's Department of Adaptive Machine Systems, believes robots should look, act, and even feel like humans. Yet Stephen Keeney, the project leader for Honda America's North American Advanced Step in Innovative Mobility (ASIMO), says they will have to look more artificial and like something out of a sci-fi movie before humans will accept them.

"The Japanese want humanoid robots, especially the elderly," says Ishiguro. "Japanese culture is very robot-centric, as they are used as toys from early childhood, and children in Japan love to play with real androids. There are even special places for androids in Japan, and they are constantly shown in cartoons and movies. Therefore, Japanese people are much more accepting of androids."

There's a different perspective in the West, where Keeney says robots aren't meant to replace human workers. "Rather," he says, "they are meant to be a machine to help make our lives better. We should always be cognizant that ASIMO is a machine and should be approachable and not be scary to children. It is a comfortable middle ground between machine and humanoid androids that others are working on."

ASIMO on the Go

Five unique processing systems control the ASIMO, and in terms of compute power, each system would rival today's top-end personal computers. Honda's engineers also had to devise complex algorithms for predictive step taking, including walking, running, running in circles, and climbing steps. This was particularly challenging because no study has ever really revealed the logic behind how humans walk, shift their weight, and avoid objects.

ASIMO is the culmination of 20 years of research and development. It uses sensors and algorithms to process moving objects and access distance and direction. For example, ASIMO stops when someone walks in front of it. Much like bats as they navigate and find prey, it also uses supersonic waves to sense movement and map its environment.

Other sensors enable ASIMO to better interact with humans. It can recognize postures and gestures, distinguish voices and sounds, identify the source of sounds, and distinguish between up to 10 different human faces. It can even address people by name.

Working in conjunction with an infrared laser beam, two visual cameras in the eyes and two infrared cameras help ASIMO find objects on the floor up to six feet away. The infrared cameras use landmarks placed on the floor so ASIMO can reposition and recalibrate itself within its environment. The markers consist of two triangles with different markings, so ASIMO can differentiate between them. It then uses itself and the two markers to triangulate its position.

Network integration lets ASIMO access the Internet and provide news, weather, and other info. It can integrate with a user's network system to access information about people at an event, show a picture of the visitor's face, and then guide visitors to their destination.

A series of actuators in the robot's joints provides 34 degrees of freedom, including three for head rotation and up/down movement, seven for each arm, two for each hand (not including joints for five bending fingers), six in each leg, and one for the torso.

ASIMO for the Elderly and Disabled

Robots must take on some human characteristics to deliver the kind of care a human counterpart provides.

"We are making a humanoid robot instead of one that runs on treads or wheels to deal with steps, doorknobs, and so on, so it can operate effectively in our world. Therefore, it needs to reflect a human form," says Keeney.

ASIMO was created with human-like arms, legs, feet, hands, and digits so it could do things like turn a doorknob to answer the door, bend its legs to lift a patient from his wheelchair, and climb stairs to find a medicine bottle—feats that robots of old couldn't accomplish.

"We are not trying to limit ourselves in the number of ways ASIMO can help," Keeney says. "ASIMO is not supposed to be a replacement for human caregivers. If you want to reach the mass market, it must be affordable. Our objective is to help people that are disabled or those who may need extra help."

While ASIMO's capabilities increase daily, such a robot is not yet within financial reach. "A lot will depend on the momentum with which technology continues to improve," says Keeney.

"As memory becomes cheaper and technology gets scaled down, ASIMO will be cheaper to manufacture. ASIMO must be smart enough to carry out commands, and we have a lot of work on artificial intelligence (AI) to make ASIMO useful in a home or hospice environment. We are probably more like 40 to 50 years from the ASIMO that can take over the household," he notes.

For now, though, Honda expects a useful version of ASIMO to be made available in about 10 years.

Honda's goal is to establish a database that contains all of the necessary information for ASIMO to function as an assistant. Most likely, such a database would include terabytes of information that would enable ASIMO to recognize voice commands and rationalize thought processes.

"The more we study AI, the more we learn what we don't know about the human brain. Every day, new challenges are emerging. We are so much in the infancy that I don't even know where to begin," says Keeney. "The more that you think about even the simplest of processes, the more you realize we rely on past experiences and common sense, and how do you write code for that?"

Challenges Ahead

Key challenges lie in improving and even perfecting interpersonal and social relationships between androids and humans. While Ishiguro and his colleagues have arguably created the world's most human-looking androids, their behaviors, facial gestures, and other body movements still need improvement.

Ishiguro also is attempting to better understand the human brain and apply cognitive science to his robots' programmed behaviors. For example, if two young women are walking next to each other and chatting, we assume they're probably friends. If two people are holding hands, we assume they're in some kind of close relationship.

Yet what is the android to conclude if a short mother and her tall son are walking together and holding hands? As humans, we would likely be able to surmise the relationship. But for androids, this task could be challenging.

Also, for instance, clearing our throats in a certain way may indicate discomfort or the need for attention. How is an android to determine when we are simply clearing our throats and when there may be some other meaning?

While there are social and moral implications to consider, Ishiguro and his colleagues first need to tackle some practical issues. For example, robots need to differentiate between individuals in large crowds of people. In one test, individual children in a large group received their own RFID [radio-frequency identification] tags, and the android had no problems identifying them.

The Uncanny Valley

Perhaps the most interesting challenge is a phenomenon known as the Uncanny Valley, theorized by Masahiro Mori in 1970. As an android's appearance and motion become more human, a human's emotional response to it becomes more positive. But this positive emotional response only increases to a point where the appearance and motions are almost too perfect and become eerie.

Then, human beings become strongly repulsed by the nearly human android. The positive response only returns when androids and humans are indistinguishable. At that point, human beings may empathize with androids as if they also were human.

Humans may be repulsed if the rate at which an android can blink its eyelids is too fast or too slow, or if it isn't smooth.

Yet if the blinking pattern matches that of an average human, we would empathize with the android. Not surprisingly, children are the first to pick up on and be repulsed by non-humanlike motions and appearances.

Just last year, Ishiguro's android's were still in the Uncanny Valley, but recent progress has changed that. "Now, with the correct number of actuators, the android has come out of the Uncanny Valley. The movements still need improvements, but the current generation is much improved," Ishiguro says.

"The young infants are now not afraid. We are still very far from replicating the exact movement of humans, and there is no way to have a perfect copy of humans within 50 years. However, with very short interactions of a minute or two, most would not know they are interacting with an android."

According to Ishiguro, human-like movement is the most important characteristic. Androids must also be able to understand answers and surmise information based on conversations. And, there's a need to research androids in real-life situations. For instance, take an android to a shopping mall and observe its behavior. Then it's back to the lab to make improvements and continue the cycle.

To better understand human behaviors and apply cognitive science, Ishiguro's team is about 50% psychologists and 50% engineers of varying fields. To improve social behaviors, the psychologists are working closely with the engineers to create algorithms that attempt to mimic the cognitive aspects.

"We are interested in making a human robot so we better understand humans," says Ishiguro. "In our search, we ask ourselves what it means to be human. This is the psychological aspect of android research. Yet there are obviously several hard sciences involved in robotics as well. So it is a great combination to learn about both humans and engineering."

Making Androids Humanoid

Now take ASIMO's underlying technologies and apply human-looking skin made of silicon with integrated piezoelectric touch sensors and plenty of actuators for controlling facial features. You'd get Hiroshi Ishiguro's Androids. Ishiguro and his fellow researchers at Osaka University want to create androids that, at first glance, are indistinguishable from the humans they resemble.

"The android is [a] communication tool. In Japan, we have a serious problem: too many old people without enough young people to entertain them. Many elderly can walk themselves, so assistance with a mechanical system can be provided with communication support. Physical support can also be provided," says Ishiguro.

"And, androids are excellent for general-purpose use with children. Androids can also provide entertainment in the form of tour guides and can be used as receptionists to explain a company and greet people as they entered the building. Androids would make good companions, and this is the most important market for the android technologies."

Robots to Carry Battle Casualties

Charles J. Murray

Charles J. Murray is a senior technical editor for Design News *magazine. In the following article he describes a humanoid robot called the Bear, for Battlefield Extraction Assist Robot. Large and strong, it is designed to rescue battlefield casualties and dispose of bombs—jobs that involve high risk when performed by live soldiers. Currently the Bear has wheels, but prototypes have been developed with jointed legs, which will enable them to ride to a battle scene, get off the vehicle, find the casualty, and load him or her onto a stretcher. In the future, such robots might also be used to move patients in hospitals. At present, the Bear is operated by remote control, but the goal is to give it autonomous intelligence so that it can sense and deal with its environment.*

Some day, you'll see videos of it rescuing battlefield casualties. Or maybe you'll pass it as it strides down a crowded hospital corridor.

Either way, you're likely to be unprepared for the first sighting of the Bear (Battlefield Extraction Assist Robot). This, after all, is no automotive paint robot. Developed by a Massachusetts-based start-up for the U.S. Army, it's only remotely related to the tens of thousands of industrial robots that have served as its ancestors. On the robotics scale, it's less like a production line assembly robot, and more like *Star Wars'* C3PO or [actor Arnold] Schwarzenegger's *Terminator.*

In many respects, it seems to be drawn straight from the annals of science fiction. Unlike its predecessors, the Bear's mobility doesn't depend on slides or gantries or rotary tables.

It has legs, knees, elbows and a face. Soon, it will squat, pick up a 250-lb man and carry him down a flight of stairs. Moreover, it can keep its balance if a wounded soldier moves in its arms. It's strong; it's smart; it's mobile; it's . . . humanoid.

"The farther we go with this, the closer it comes to a human android-type form," notes Gary Gilbert, chief of knowledge engineering for the U.S. Army Telemedicine and Technology Research Center. "The humanoid form has certain characteristics that enable it to do a lot of things we want to do. It turns out maybe evolution knew what it was doing."

Serving a Market Gap

More than three years in the making, the Bear has indeed adopted the humanoid form, and it's looking more human all the time. U.S. Army engineers say they wanted those human characteristics because the battlefield tasks it will perform require agility and strength. Initially, those tasks will include rescuing battlefield casualties and disposing of bombs—operations that are better done by robots than by live soldiers.

"It needs to get to a site, perform its mission, return safely, and protect casualties from threats in the environment," Gilbert says.

Although the Bear now uses wheels for mobility, its current prototype employs jointed track-based legs, which will enable it to carry out next-level tasks. Those include attaching itself to a ground vehicle, riding out to a battle scene, getting off the vehicle, finding the casualty, and loading him or her onto a stretcher for evacuation.

Daniel Theobald, president of Vecna Technologies Inc., says he invented the Bear robot because he saw a gap in the mobile robotics marketplace. The market, he says, was made up of two broad classes of robots: small "virtual presence robots" that could scoot beneath a car while searching for bombs; and large, remotely operated vehicles, including tanks and drones.

"We saw a real vacuum between them," Theobald says. "There was a need for a robot that could go into tight spaces—in buildings and up stairs, where vehicles can't go. But, at the same time, there was also a need for that robot to be strong enough to manipulate the environment."

Theobald foresaw his new robot being able to lift hundreds of pounds, thus exceeding the strength of small mobile robots, which typically cannot lift more than about seven pounds. By endowing the robot with such strength, Theobald believed it could fill an important niche—hoisting wounded soldiers, lifting small vehicles, rescuing civilians during nuclear or biological attacks, and checking for bombs beneath the carcasses of dead animals. He even foresaw it being used in hospital settings, where it could move patients in their beds and aid amputees or the elderly.

"You have to be strong in order to manipulate the environment in a significant way," Theobald says. "You need the ability to pick up people, move rubble, or even lift a car to help someone who's trapped."

Making that happen, however, was no small engineering feat. To accomplish it, Theobald considered it critical that the robot use hydraulics to power its upper body. He employed 1,500-psi [pounds per square inch] hydraulic cylinders from Quincy Ortman Cylinders, fed by valves from HydraForce Inc. Vecna's engineering team also custom-designed an orientation-independent hydraulic reservoir for the system, mainly so that hydraulic fluid wouldn't spill from the robot when it bent down or assumed an unusual position. The hydraulic system enables the Bear's upper arms and torso to lift approximately 400 pounds.

"There's definitely a trade-off to using hydraulics," says Theobald, whose graduate work at MIT [Massachusetts Institute of Technology] included developing Web-based control algorithms for a robotic Mars explorer. "Hydraulic systems are fairly heavy and you pay a penalty for that. But the benefit is that you can get all the power into one joint at one time. Whereas, if you distributed electric motors around the robot, you would only get what's available from each individual motor. To get equal power, you would need huge electric motors."

Learning Balance

Even as it lifts massive weights, however, the Bear faces a separate challenge: balance. To keep it from tipping as it lifts a wounded soldier, steps over a log, or walks down a hill, the Bear's engineers also employed dynamic balancing.

"When you scale down the footprint of a robot while keeping it fairly massive, you end up with a balance problem," Theobald says.

Dynamic balancing addressed that issue by keeping the robot's center of gravity over its legs (or wheels, as the case may be). Much like a human, the Bear had to learn to shift its weight while standing. If it tipped forward, it had to learn to lean back to place its center of gravity over its feet. Conversely, if it tipped backward, it had to lean forward.

To accomplish that, Theobald and robotics product manager, Jamie Nichol, incorporated sensors that enable the Bear to keep track of its limbs, torso and legs. A torso-based inertial measurement unit from SpaceAge Control Inc. detects the robot's attitude, while optical joint encoders from U.S. Digital track angular displacement of body parts. Signals from the encoders are sent to 21 PIC microcontrollers from Microchip Technology, Inc., which are incorporated in the robot's joints. Joint microcontrollers are segregated into five sub-networks: left arm; right arm; left leg; right leg; and torso.

"We wanted to give every joint its own smarts," notes Jamie Nichol, whose Ph.D. work at Stanford [University] included mechatronics and kinematics. "By doing that, we reduced the amount of network traffic in the robot."

Reducing that network traffic was critical, Vecna engineers say, because the robot employs a central computer that must perform the highest level chores. The Linux-based central processing computer, an EPIA-M [embedded platform innovative architecture M series] motherboard from Via Technologies, does the more intense computing, including running the custom-designed balancing algorithms and high-level coordination programs. Based on decisions made by those programs, the CPU [central processing unit] sends signals to the microcontrollers at the nodes, which "talk" to the motors, valves, and other actuators that power the robot.

The Bear's legs, or wheels, also take direction from microcontrollers located at the knees and hips. While early versions of the Bear have employed wheels for movement, current prototypes incorporate four motor-driven tracks. The tracks—located above and below the knees on each leg—are powered by a 2HP [horsepower] brush-type permanent magnet from MagMotor Corp., through a planetary gearbox reduction. In essence, the tracks form the robot's legs, enabling it to stand straight up and walk, climb stairs, or step over obstacles.

"We designed two independent legs with tracks, so it's able to crawl up the stairs while maintaining positive contact with the top of every stair," Theobald says. By doing so, the massive robot doesn't break off a chunk of stairway as it ascends or descends. "Obviously, when you're carrying a human being, you don't want to take risks you don't need to take," he says.

Next Challenge: Autonomy

For reasons such as those, U.S. Army engineers say they're pleased with the humanoid configuration of the Bear.

"A lot of people said, 'You don't need that,'" says Gilbert of the U.S. Army. "They told us, 'Just use four wheels or a forklift.' But it turns out those forms can't negotiate stairs; they can't corner sharply enough; and they're not gentle enough."

Gilbert adds that the Army also hopes to endow future Bear-type robots with autonomous intelligence. Today, he says, the Bear is still tele-operated through remote control.

Eventually, though, Army engineers hope to use laser, radar and sonar-type sensors to give future robots the ability to sense, understand and deal with their environments.

"Robots are still in their infancy," Gilbert says. "And autonomy is still the biggest challenge in robotics."

For now, though, the Bear's engineers have succeeded in attaining the program's first two goals: proof-of-concept and the ability to climb stairs. It can now stand up on its jointed, track-style legs and run. In the near future, however, there is still a long list of goals: react to unexpected obstacles; run sideways down a hill; sense the environment around it.

"The ultimate objective of this program is complete autonomy," Gilbert says. "And the only way to get there is to start, and that's what we've done."

Robots as Future Space Explorers

Paul Levinson

Paul Levinson is a professor and the chair of the Communication and Media Studies Department at Fordham University. He is the author of many books, both nonfiction and science fiction. In this excerpt from his nonfiction book Realspace: The Fate of Physical Presence in the Digital Age, On and Off Planet, *he considers the issue of whether humanoid robots would make better space explorers than humans. Sending robots alone into space would avoid risking lives. Robots, however, would have neither the experience nor the emotions that would be needed for interpreting unpredictable aspects of what they encountered in unknown environments. Perhaps, in the distant future, robots with emotions might be created. But if they were enough like humans to have human emotions, Levinson argues, then the risk to them would be no more acceptable than risk to human life—which negates the main advantage of using robots instead of people to explore new worlds.*

The first and foremost advantage of robots over humans as explorers of space is that the loss of a robot is at worst a severe inconvenience of time and money—it is not a loss of life. Here on Earth, in environments in which we already know, and know to be dangerous, use of robots certainly makes sense. If we could construct a robot to mix dangerous chemicals, or biological materials, what logic would there be in insisting that human beings do the job?

There are also some lesser benefits of robot workers, which might well commend them as explorers. Robots don't get bored with repetitive tasks. They don't miss family back home, don't fall in love with co-workers, don't get angry, annoyed, distracted with any of the myriad concerns, small and monumental, petty and wonderful, to which we humans are prone. In short, robots partake of all the advantages of strictly logical, unemotional artificial intelligences—computers—that operate wholly on the basis of programs and circuits not hormones.

The combination of such advantages—real, if difficult to calculate—along with the cardinal benefit of robots not having a life to lose, make an undeniable case for major robotic participation in our engagement of the solar system and its worlds and moons. But should this participation be to the exclusion of flesh-and-blood humans?

The answer would certainly be yes, as long as there were no significant advantages of humans over robots in space. The fact that a human has a life to lose, and a robot does not, is clearly a weighty argument against sending a human to do a robot's possible job.

But does being alive—being fully human—also have some irreducible advantages for the job of emissary to the stars?

Limitations of Programming

Behavioral psychologists such as B.F. Skinner once argued that humans are no less programmed than machines—any difference resides in our unawareness of our programming (that is, we are aware that we have programmed the machine, but are unaware that we have been programmed by our past experience, the unawareness of the machine or computer of its programming by us is not at issue). [Artificial intelligence expert] Marvin Minsky made a similar point when he referred to our brains as "meat machines"—by which he meant the significant difference between our brains and computers is that we are constructed of protein and computer chips of silicon, but both run on programs. (A similar perspective animates the distinction between cyberspace and "meat-space." The latter refers to what I have been calling "real-space" in [my] book, but seeks to deprive it of any privileged position in human affairs over cyberspace. I prefer my appellation "realspace" precisely because it calls attention to that position.)

Characterizations such as Skinner's and Minsky's are often presented as alternatives to the religious notion that we—our brains and bodies—are somehow charged by an ineffable soul, or the philosophic contention (from [seventeenth-century philosopher René] Descartes and many others) that our brains are driven by, and/or give rise to, our nonmaterial minds. In the homogenized programmed mindset, thought and dreams and schemes and if/then algorithm routines are indistinguishable in their essential nature.

But the claim that human mentalities are totally the product of programming, in the same sense as a computer's (or robot's) decisions, can be refuted with recourse to neither soul nor mind. The plain fact is that the human adult has had experiences which verge on the infinite in comparison to anything programmable into a computer, and these human experiences play upon genetic "programs" in the brain—such as our capacity to communicate via language—that are themselves vast and barely charted at present. Thus, even if we want to accept, for the sake of discussion, that human mental operations are "programmed," there is no meaningful equation or even comparison between that kind of human programming, and what we do with computers. The scales of relevant programmable variables are in two different universes.

For all intents and purposes, then, human beings are in effect "unprogrammed" in comparison to computers. Imagine a person standing on a new world, or looking at it from a hovercraft, for the first time—or, for that matter, a second, third, hundredth, or thousandth time. Think about what this visitor might see after a moment, an hour, a decade, a lifetime of observation on this new planet. Perhaps some nuance of movement, some flicker of pattern, that might resonate with something she saw when she was 5 years old, walking to school, playing in a garden, climbing a fence, back on Earth. Maybe a ripple in the new world's water, a bend of a leaf, that recalls something she saw when running with her friends by a lake in the park when she was 11. Or perhaps the glint of the sun in this distant solar system, bouncing off a mountain for an instant in the morning, that conveys something of her grandmother's smile.

Does this last example, especially, take an unfair shot at computers? Does it have little discernible connection to scientific inquiry? That is exactly the point. Scouts need more than rigorous scientific education. They also need wellsprings of unspecified emotion and experience, the better to match up with who knows what may be encountered out there in space. What computer program embedded in a robot's brain could possibly encompass such experience?

This near infinity of uncataloged experience that all humans carry is a friend to discovery. The key difference between humans and robots on this point is not that our minds are more specifically prepared than robot programs to recognize important details and events. Rather, our advantage comes in what we have not been prepared for—in the plethora of experience of just living and thinking. If [ancient Greek philosopher] Plato is right in his "Meno" paradox that we cannot learn anything new unless we already know something of it— for how else would we recognize the new as knowledge at all—then the grab-bag of life is surely indispensable packing for voyages of discovery in space.

And we humans have other advantages over robots.

Knowledge in Tiers and Tears

The three traditional branches of philosophy ask what is true and false (epistemology), right and wrong (ethics), beautiful and ugly (aesthetics). Computers may be programmed to make decisions about all three, but are on weakest grounds in the third area. Facts of course can be stored in digital, non-organic forms, and accessed by programs which can then tender informed decisions about whether new data are true or false, this can certainly be of assistance in epistemology. Ethics are more difficult, but amenable, to some extent, to if/then programs. A computer "judge" could consider: If a man's 3-year-old daughter is in need of urgent medical attention, should the man be permitted to exceed the speed limit to rush her to the hospital? Suitably stocked with if/then guidelines and examples—if medical needs are sufficiently urgent, then traffic rules can be violated—we could have confidence that our AI [artificial intelligence] magistrate would make the right decision.

But aesthetics? A robot might well be programmed with an immense store of images and sounds that humans have judged to be beautiful. But would we then trust it to recognize even a slightly new form of beauty?

The problem is that the principles of aesthetics are poorly understood even for humans—sorting through facts and weighing of ethics primarily entail thinking (though some feeling or emotion may be involved in ethics), but objects of beauty are felt (apprehended by emotions, as some old-time philosopher might have said), with perhaps some thought involved. So beauty is quite the opposite from truth and right in the blend of intellect and emotion it requires to be perceived and assessed.

Consider the plight of the robot looking out at some desolate landscape in some faraway part of the galaxy. The very word "desolate" underlines the robot's problem. Presumably the robot could give us a factually accurate report of the paucity of stars, planets, mountains, whatever, in the area—how many it observed, and how closely packed. Our robot might also make an ethically sound decision. Say, if a human explorer died, and uttered nothing before dying, our robot might be programmed to nonetheless tell the explorer's husband back on Earth that she said she loved him just before she died. But what could our robot report—what could it know—about the aesthetic state of "desolate"?

Could it convey anything of [seventeenth-century philosopher Blaise] Pascal's sense of the awesome disproportion, the minuscularity, of our minds, brains, dreams, our existence, in comparison to the immensity of the Universe? Could it know the awe that we feel right here on Earth when we look out at the starry skies? Not likely. No, not at all. Our robot might well know of *our* awe, and the circumstances that call it forth. Our robot might notice something different in our eyes when we look up at the Universe from this Earth and try to fathom what it all means. Our robot might well be programmed to recognize similar circumstances in other places—jet-black nights agleam with silent stars over deserts or tundra on other planets—and tell us about them. But to know the awe itself, to know the sense of desolation, would require feeling, experiencing the awe—and that, in turn, requires emotions, or brains bartended by adrenaline and other hormones. Can logic circuits be bathed by hormones—meaningfully "interface" with them (to use that awkward verb)? Perhaps, someday. But certainly we have no robots or computer programs which feel that way today.

And the presence of human emotions on the cutting edges of our expeditions in space is no mere luxury. How many times have you walked into a house or an apartment you were thinking of buying or renting, highly recommended by a friend or agent and/or looking great on paper, and, as soon as you were inside, you realized that it was not right for you? How many times have you had the same experience with an automobile you were considering purchasing? These decisions are based on more than knowledge, facts, information. They entail emotional responses, sometimes so minute as to be unconscious, or incapable of articulation. And yet—certainly in the case of a new home—they can guide the most important decisions of our lives.

Don't we need every bit of this as we consider new homes in space?

Robots with Emotions?

But if we are thinking about distant futures, might we not be able at that time to build robots with emotions? It isn't so hard to imagine—indeed, it's been imagined many times in science fiction literature, and well portrayed on the screen.

If we were able to someday construct robots to not only reason, but feel, would these robots be subject to the entire range of human emotions? Anything less would still count against them as our sole envoys to the stars, for we would be hard-pressed to know just which of our emotions were most needed for interstellar excursions. And creation of robots with full ranges of human emotions would presumably be more daunting than building of robots with only some emotions. The portrayal of robots and androids (robots that look like humans) in motion pictures and on television actually makes such a task—the creation of fully "feeling" robots, with computer programs capable of complete aesthetic responses—appear far more easy to accomplish than it probably will be. Human actors and actresses are, after all, portraying the androids, so any emotion we may see in the androids is a function not of the android (which of course does not really exist as yet) but the face of the human actor or actress (which of course really does exist).

Specialists in nonverbal communication have cataloged hundreds of different smiles, smile/eye combinations, and so forth on the human face. Most of us not only make, but recognize and understand, most of those intricate, subtle expressions. A robot could probably be programmed in the recognition, even the rendering of the expressions seems not beyond sufficiently sophisticated android construction. The catch is that each expression, for us, reflects an internal mental state—an aesthetic or other emotional response. What would the expressions reflect in a robot?

But let us assume, for argument's sake, that we will some-day be able to construct robots with the entire panoply of hu-man emotions. Would such entities then be preferable to hu-mans as our sole emissaries to the stars—that is, could we be comfortable with their observations and reports and on-site analyses and decisions, in our human absence? Equating emo-tions with souls for a moment (or souls with a mixture of cognition and profoundest feeling which characterize our humanity), and putting aside the religious question of how souls come to be in the first place (for we could say that, if only the Supreme Being can breathe souls into humans, then these robots were so human in every other way that the Su-preme Being might have seen fit to invest them with souls), would robots with such "souls" make satisfactory sole en-voys—soul envoys—to the Universe?

Sadly, no. And not because such robots, on this account, would still be less than human. The problem with robots "who" were human in every important way and went to the stars on our behalves arises from just the opposite—the fact that such hypothetical robots would not be different enough from us. The one undeniable advantage of any robot, as we saw above, is that we can feel comfortable risking its existence before that of a human being. No one likes to lose a car or an expensive computer, but only a lunatic would hold such losses equal to that of a human being. So, if we make robots so hu-man that they can survey the Universe in our complete ab-sence, without any detriment to the results of the survey, are we not therein making their loss—their "death," perhaps—no less unacceptable than ours?

A Fundamental Paradox

We may think of this as a fundamental, unavoidable paradoxical "principle" of robotic substitution for human beings: the more like humans they become, the less acceptable their exposure to danger, injury, death, and, the less like humans they remain, the less reliable their reports about places we have never seen or experienced first-hand. This limitation gets us and our robots coming and going. It counts against their use as our sole emissaries at all stages of their development, primitive and present and real, as well as future.

Science fiction, for the most part, has focused on the dangers robots may pose to us, not what perils we might visit on them. [Science Fiction author] Isaac Asimov's "three laws of robotics"—a robot may never through action or inaction cause harm, or permit it to come, to a human; a robot must follow all human orders, except when they contradict the first law; a robot must act in its own self-defense, except when such actions might contradict the first two laws—are an excellent example: a robot's well being comes last, even subsidiary to a moronic or malicious human order to jump off the roof, for no reason other than that the human has commanded this. (Asimov later posited a "zeroth" law, to take precedence over the first, which insisted that the good of humanity as a whole outweighed the needs of any human individual. This could allow a robot to kill a person on behalf of humanity. But the new law was no help to robots, whose "rights" were still in last place.)

But the more intelligent, profound and sensitive we build our robots—the better able they may be to implement Asimov's laws—the more in need of protection they themselves become from us. Because they have become, or are becoming, us.

All things considered, then, we may have to settle for low-grade robots—low-grade in terms of science fiction, high-tech in terms of what we may actually now or soon produce—to accompany us to the stars. They present us with no ethical dilemmas in their loss as they help us with whatever tasks we assign to them. The only danger we court in their use is assuming they can make decisions, fully explore worlds, in our absence.

Humanoid Robots Cannot Replace Humans

David Bruemmer

David Bruemmer is a computer scientist working at the Idaho National Laboratory, which supports the U.S. Department of Energy. In the following viewpoint he discusses what interaction with humanoid robots will mean to human society. Humanoids will never replace humans, he says; rather, they will enable the exploration and further realization of human nature. To be useful, they must be able to adapt and develop, and that will require them to have motivation, which may or may not be called emotion. Whether their emotions and/or intelligence can be considered "real" is less important than the effect they have on people. Robots are not likely to seize control of the world, but people may give it to them, one step at a time, by gradually becoming more and more dependent on their existence. "Pulling the plug" may become as unthinkable as it would now be to disable the Internet.

Few technologies capture the human imagination quite like humanoid robots. Like many new technologies, today's early humanoids are primarily used as research tools and sometimes as costly curiosities for entertainment. However, in time, they will accomplish a wide variety of tasks in homes, battlefields, nuclear plants, government installations, factory floors, and even space stations. Perhaps more importantly, they will change the way we spend our time, the way we view technology, the way we understand our own minds and bodies and the characteristics we value in each other.

Humanoids will exhibit emotion, forge relationships, make decisions, and develop as they learn through interaction with

David Bruemmer, "Humanoid Robotics: Ethical Considerations," *Idaho National Laboratory*, May 30, 2006. Copyright © 2006 David Bruemmer. Reproduced by permission of author.

the environment. Already, humanoid robots can carry out high-level commands given through gesture and speech and can adapt and orchestrate existing behaviors using a variety of machine learning techniques. While these capabilities are important steps, useful, general-purpose functionality remains an elusive goal. One of the implications of current research is that to create human-like adaptability and versatility, it may be necessary to introduce an element of human-like frailty and inconsistency. Human resourcefulness derives, at least in part, from our ability to use the arbitrary fluctuations in ourselves and our environment to drive learning, creativity, and inventiveness. Like humans, robots cannot learn if they are not allowed to make mistakes. The future will bring humanoids designed not for optimality, but rather to take part in the drama of chaos, inconsistency and error we know as the real world.

The world's population of real humans continues to steadily grow. One might ask why we would want to make a human-like machine when we have plenty of humans already, many of whom do not have jobs or good places to live. It is important to emphasize that humanoid roboticists do not intend to recreate or replace humans. Robots and humans are good at fundamentally different things. Calculators did not replace mathematicians. They did drastically change the way mathematics was taught. For example, the ability to mentally multiply large numbers, although impressive, is no longer a highly valued human capability. Calculators have not stolen from us part of what it means to be human, but rather, free our minds for more worthy efforts. As humanoids change the contours of our workforce, economy and society, they will not displace us, but may enable us to further realize the very aspects of our nature we hold most dear.

If the goal is not to replicate humans, why are roboticists trying to create robots that can exhibit and respond to emotion? Emotion is often considered a debilitating, irrational characteristic. Why not keep humanoids, like calculators, merely as useful gadgetry? Since humans already use emotive cues to guide interaction, it stands to reason that robots intended to interact with them will benefit from the ability to perceive, exhibit and respond to these cues. At another level, emotion can be viewed not simply as a communication aid, but as something which underlies intelligence, providing intrinsic motivation and intentionality. For those working to develop imitative learning for humanoids, the question of how to motivate and modulate development is a profound question. Speaking in utilitarian terms, emotion is the implementation of a motivational system that propels us to work, improve, reproduce and survive. In robots, we may choose to call this system "emotion" or we may reserve that term for ourselves and assert that humanoids are merely using human programming to simulate emotion.

Most likely, two distinct species of humanoids will arise: those that respond to and ellicit our emotions and those we wish simply to do work, day in and day out, without stirring our feelings. Some ethicists believe this may be a difficult distinction to maintain. On the other hand, many consider ethical concerns regarding robot emotion or intelligence to be moot. According to this line of reasoning, no robot really feels or knows anything that we have not (albeit indirectly) told them to feel or know. From this perspective, it seems unnecessary to give a second thought to our treatment of humanoids. They are not "real." They are merely machines.

At their onset, all technologies seem artificial, and upset the perceived natural way of things. With the rise of the Internet, we coined the notion of a "virtual world" as a means to distinguish a new, unfamiliar arena from our usual daily life. However, to someone who spends 10 hours a day logged into Internet chat rooms, the so-called "virtual world" is as real to them as anything else in their lives. Likewise, the interactions humans have with humanoids will be real because we make them so. Many years from now, our grandchildren will be puzzled by the question, "Does the robot have 'real' intelligence?" Intelligence is as intelligence does. As we hone them, enable them to self-develop, integrate them into our lives and become comfortable with them, humanoids will seem (and be) less and less contrived. Ultimately, the most relevant issue is not whether a robot's emotion or intelligence can be considered "real," but rather the fact that, real or not, it will have an effect on us.

If it is hard to imagine how humans could develop an emotional connection to a robot, consider what the effects would be of systematically imparting knowledge, personality and intentions to a robot over a sustained period of time. Even if the public is not given the ability to modify source code, humanoids will develop and learn in response to the input they receive. Could a cruel master make a cruel humanoid? Will people begin to see their robots as a reflection of themselves? As works of art? As valuable tools? As children? If humanoids learn "bad behavior," whom should we hold responsible? The manufacturer? The owner? The robot? Or the surrounding environment as a collective whole? The ethical questions of nature vs. nurture are relevant for humanoids as well as humans. It will be hard enough to monitor the software and mechanical "nature" of humanoids (i.e. the state in which humanoids emerge from the factory crate). "Nurture" presents an even greater challenge.

As they develop, it may well be that no two humanoids are the same. The random variations in themselves and the environment may eventually lead to creativity, innovation and even humor. Some humans may argue indefinitely about whether the robots have "true" intelligence, will, or emotion. Regardless, the majority of us will project these traits into them anyway. We will watch as humanoids do things our own bodies do not allow and will observe their power run out and see their bodies malfunction. We will know that they are not human and yet this fact will not preclude emotional involvement. Even those who consider humanoids to be mere machines will find themselves responding differently to one humanoid than another. Humans are so well versed in the art of lopsided communication that we can pour affection on automobiles or even inert objects. How much easier will it be to develop a relationship with a humanoid that makes you laugh and listens to you when no one else is willing.

The primary concern is not that humanoids will become super intelligent or that they will take over the world. The consequences of their introduction will be subtler. Inexorably, we will interact more with machines and less with each other. Already, the average American worker spends astonishingly large percentages of his/her workday interfacing with machines. Many return home only to log in anew. Human relationships are a lot of trouble, forged from dirty diapers, lost tempers and late nights. Machines, on the other hand, can be turned on and off. Already, many of us prefer to forge and maintain relationships via e-mail, chat rooms and instant messenger rather than in person. Despite promises that the Internet will take us anywhere, we find ourselves—hour after hour—glued to our chairs. We are supposedly living in a world with no borders. Yet, at the very time we should be coming closer together, it seems we are growing further apart. Humanoids may accelerate this trend.

Whatever else it may be, technological progress flows with a swift current. One lesson to be learned from the Internet, which continues to grow rapidly with little oversight, is that the better a technology, the more dependent we become upon it. As technology becomes more pervasive, complex and dangerous, we will be ever more likely to employ the aid of humanoids. Most likely, humanoids will never rise up and wrest control from our hands. Instead, we may give it to them, one home, one factory, one nuclear facility at a time until "pulling the plug" becomes, at first infeasible and then eventually unthinkable. Imagine an attempt to "pull the plug" on the Internet. Once it is out of the box, it is difficult to revoke a technology without incurring profound economic, social and psychological consequences.

Yet, no matter how quickly technological progress seems to unfold, foresight and imagination will always play key roles in driving societal change. We cannot shirk responsibility by calling the future inevitable. It is difficult to direct a snowball as it careens down the slope; thus, it is now—when there are only a handful of functional humanoids around the world— that we must decide the direction in which to push. Humanoids are the products of our own minds and hands. Neither we, nor our creations, stand outside the natural world, but rather are an integral part of its unfolding. We have designed humanoids to model and extend aspects of ourselves and, if we fear them, it is because we fear ourselves.

CHAPTER 4

AI That Equals
or Surpasses
Human Intelligence

Machines with Human Intelligence Will Soon Be Built

Ray Kurzweil

Ray Kurzweil is an inventor, futurist, and the author of five books. He is among today's most outspoken proponents of the view that machine intelligence will soon surpass human intelligence. In the following selection he summarizes past ideas about robots, then explains the advances being made in understanding the human brain. In Kurzweil's opinion, scientists are coming closer and closer to knowledge of how the mind works, and the speed of this progress will increase. He believes that once the complexity of the brain has been analyzed, it will be possible to program computers—even inexpensive computers—that are thousands of times as powerful as human brains, and that human-level intelligence in machines will be achieved by the year 2029. Also by then, he says, androids that are fully human-like can be created, and at the same time human bodies will be augmented by blood-cell-size robots, so that the boundary between humans and machines will be transcended.

Human experience is marked by a refusal to obey our limitations. We've escaped the ground, we've escaped the planet, and now, after thousands of years of effort, our quest to build machines that emulate our own appearance, movement and intelligence is leading us to the point where we will escape the two most fundamental confines of all: our bodies and our minds. Once this point comes—once the accelerating pace of technological change allows us to build machines that not only equal but surpass human intelligence—we'll see cyborgs (machine-enhanced humans like the *Six Million Dollar Man*), androids (human-robot hybrids like Data in *Star Trek*) and other combinations beyond what we can even imagine.

Although the ancient Greeks were among the first to build machines that could emulate the intelligence and natural movements of people (developments invigorated by the Greeks' musings that human intelligence might also be governed by natural laws), these efforts flowered in the European Renaissance, which produced the first androids with lifelike movements. These included a mandolin-playing lady, constructed in 1540 by Italian inventor Gianello Torriano. In 1772 Swiss watchmaker Pierre Jacquet-Droz built a pensive child named L'Écrivain (The Writer) that could write passages with a pen. L'Écrivian's brain was a mechanical computer that was impressive for its complexity even by today's standards.

Such inventions led scientists and philosophers to speculate that the human brain itself was just an elaborate automaton. [German philosopher and mathematician] Wilhelm Leibniz, a contemporary of [English physicist and mathematician] Isaac Newton, wrote around 1700: "What if these theories are really true, and we were magically shrunk and put into someone's brain while he was thinking. We would see all the pumps, pistons, gears and levers working away, and we would be able to describe their workings completely, in mechanical terms, thereby completely describing the thought processes of the brain. But that description would nowhere contain any mention of thought! It would contain nothing but descriptions of pumps, pistons, levers!"

Leibniz was on to something. There are indeed pumps, pistons and levers inside our brain—we now recognize them as neurotransmitters, ion channels and the other molecular components of the neural machinery. And although we don't yet fully understand the details of how these little machines create thought, our ignorance won't last much longer.

The Idea of Robots

The word "robot" originated almost a century ago. Czech dramatist Karel Capek first used the term in his 1921 play *R.U.R.*

(for "Rossum's Universal Robots"), creating it from the Czech word "robota," meaning obligatory work. In the play, he describes the invention of intelligent biomechanical machines intended as servants for their human creators. While lacking charm and goodwill, his robots brought together all the elements of machine intelligence: vision, touch sensitivity, pattern recognition, decision making, world knowledge, fine motor coordination and even a measure of common sense.

Capek intended his intelligent machines to be evil in their perfection, their perfect rationality scornful of human frailty. These robots ultimately rise up against their masters and destroy all humankind, a dystoplan notion that has been echoed in much science fiction since.

The specter of machine intelligence enslaving its creators has continued to impress itself on the public consciousness. But more significantly, Capek's robots introduced the idea of the robot as an imitation or substitute for a human being. The idea has been reinforced throughout the 20th century, as androids engaged the popular imagination in fiction and film, from Rosle to C-3PO and the Terminator.

The first generation of modern robots were, however, a far cry from these anthropomorphic visions, and most robot builders have made no attempt to mimic humans. The Unimate, a popular assembly-line robot from the 1960s, was capable only of moving its one arm in several directions and opening and closing its gripper. Today there are more than two million Roomba robots scurrying around, performing a task (vacuuming) that used to be done by humans, but they look more like fast turtles than maids. Most robots will continue to be utilitarian devices designed to carry out specific tasks. But when we think of the word "robot," Capek's century-old concept of machines made in our own image still dominates our imagination and inspires our goals.

The aspiration to build human-level androids can be regarded as the ultimate challenge in artificial intelligence. To do it, we need to understand not just human cognition but also our physical skill—it is, after all, a critical part of what the brain does. Coordinating intention with movement in a complex environment is largely the responsibility of the cerebellum, which comprises more than half the neurons in the brain. And the body itself represents much of our complexity: There is more information in the human genome, which describes the human body, than in the design of the brain.

Understanding the Brain

We are making tremendous strides toward being able to understand how the brain works. The performance/price ratio, capacity and bandwidth of every type of information technology, electronic and biological alike, is doubling about every year. I call this pervasive phenomenon the law of accelerating returns. Our grasp of biology is proceeding at an accelerating pace, also exponentially increasing every year. It took scientists five years to be able to sequence HIV, for example, but the SARS [severe acute respiratory syndrome], virus required only 31 days. The amount of genetic data that's been sequenced has doubled every year since the human genome project began in 1990, and the cost per base pair has come down by half each year, from $10 in 1990 to about a penny today. We are making comparable gains in understanding how the genome expresses itself in proteins and in understanding how a broad range of biological mechanisms work. Indeed, we are augmenting and re-creating nearly every organ and system in the human body: hearts and pancreases, joints and muscles.

The same progression applies to our knowledge of the human brain. The three-dimensional resolution of brain scans has been exponentially increasing, and the latest generation of scanners can image individual neuronal connections firing in real time. The amount of data that scientists are gathering on the brain is similarly increasing every year. And they are showing that this information can be understood by converting it into models and simulations of brain regions, some two dozen of which have already been completed. IBM also recently began an ambitious effort to model a substantial part of the cerebral cortex in incredible detail.

If we are to re-create the powers of the human brain, we first need to understand how complex it is. There are 100 billion neurons, each with thousands of connections and each connection containing about 1,000 neural pathways. I've estimated the amount of information required to characterize the state of a mature brain at thousands of trillions of bytes: a lot of complexity.

But the design of the brain is a billion times as simple as this. How do we know? The design of the human brain—and body—is stored in the genome, and the genome doesn't contain that much information. There are three billion rungs of DNA in the human genome: six billion bits, or 800 million bytes. It is replete with redundancies, however; one lengthy sequence called ALU is repeated 300,000 times. Since we know the genome's structure, we can compress its information to only 30 million to 100 million bytes, which is smaller than the code for Microsoft Word. About half of this contains the design of the human brain.

The brain can be described in just 15 million to 50 million bytes because most of its wiring is random at birth. For example, the trillions of connections in the cerebellum are described by only a handful of genes. This means that most of the cerebellum wiring in the infant brain is chaotic. The system is designed to be self-organizing, though, so as the child learns to walk and talk and catch a fly ball, the cerebellum gets filled with meaningful information.

Human-Level Machine Intelligence by 2029

My point is not that the brain is simple, but that the design is at a level of complexity that we can fathom and manage. And by applying the law of accelerating returns to the problem of analyzing the brain's complexity, we can reasonably forecast that there will be exhaustive models and simulations of all several hundred regions of the human brain within about 20 years.

Once we understand how the mind operates, we will be able to program detailed descriptions of these principles into inexpensive computers, which, by the late 2020s, will be thousands of times as powerful as the human brain—another consequence of the law of accelerating returns. So we will have both the hardware and software to achieve human-level intelligence in a machine by 2029. We will also by then be able to construct fully humanlike androids at exquisite levels of detail and send blood-cell-size robots into our bodies and brains to keep us healthy from inside and to augment our intellect. By the time we succeed in building such machines, we will have become part machine ourselves. We will, in other words, finally transcend what we have so long thought of as the ultimate limitations: our bodies and minds.

Duplicating Human Intelligence Is a Mirage

Peter Kassan

In the following viewpoint, computer scientist Peter Kassan argues that the claim that computers can duplicate human intelligence is wholly unrealistic, and that in terms of what is now known of the brain, this will never happen. The more that has been learned about neuroscience, the more impossible it appears that such a goal can be reached. A model of the brain, Kassan says, would have to be at least 25 million times larger than the largest software product ever created. In addition, the approaches so far taken to artificial intelligence are based on fundamental fallacies. The history of the field, in his opinion, can be summed up as involving, first, grand theoretical visions; next, some promising early results; then a half-century of stagnation; and currently, grand promises for the future that are based on illusion.

On March 24, 2005 an announcement was made in newspapers across the country, from the *New York Times* to the *San Francisco Chronicle*, that a company had been founded to apply neuroscience research to achieve human-level artificial intelligence. The reason the press release was so widely picked up is that the man behind it was Jeff Hawkins, the brilliant inventor of the PalmPilot, an invention that made him both wealthy and respected.

You'd think from the news reports that the idea of approaching the pursuit of artificial human-level intelligence by modeling the brain was a novel one. Actually, a Web search for "computational neuroscience" finds over a *hundred thousand* webpages and several major research centers. At least two

Peter Kassan, "A.I. Gone Awry: The Futile Quest for Artificial Intelligence," *Skeptic*, vol. 12, 2006. Copyright © 2006 Skeptics Society, authors and artists. Reproduced by permission.

journals are devoted to the subject. Over 6,000 papers are available online. Amazon lists more than 50 books about it. A Web search for "human brain project" finds more than *eighteen thousand* matches. Many researchers think of modeling the human brain or creating a "virtual" brain a feasible project, even if a "grand challenge." In other words, the idea isn't a new one.

Hawkins' approach sounds simple. Create a machine with artificial "senses" and then allow it to learn, build a model of its world, see analogies, make predictions, solve problems, and give us their solutions. This sounds eerily similar to what [mathematician] Alan Turing suggested in 1948. He, too, proposed to create an artificial "man" equipped with senses and an artificial brain that could "roam the countryside," like Frankenstein's monster, and learn whatever it needed to survive.

The fact is, we have no unifying theory of neuroscience. We don't know what to build, much less how to build it. As one observer put it, neuroscience appears to be making "anti-progress"—the more information we acquire, the less we seem to know. Thirty years ago, the estimated number of neurons was between three and ten billion. Nowadays, the estimate is 100 billion. Thirty years ago it was assumed that the brain's glial cells, which outnumber neurons by nine times, were purely structural and had no other function. In 2004, it was reported that this wasn't true.

Even the most ardent artificial intelligence (A.I.) advocates admit that, so far at least, the quest for human-level intelligence has been a total failure. Despite its checkered history, however, Hawkins concludes A.I. will happen: "Yes, we can build intelligent machines."

A Brief History of A.I.

Duplicating or mimicking human-level intelligence is an old notion—perhaps as old as humanity itself. In the 19th century, as Charles Babbage conceived of ways to mechanize calculation, people started thinking it was possible—or arguing that it wasn't. Toward the middle of the 20th century, as mathematical geniuses Claude Shannon, Norbert Wiener, John von Neumann, Alan Turing, and others laid the foundations of the theory of computing, the necessary tool seemed available.

In 1955, a research project on artificial intelligence was proposed; a conference the following summer is considered the official inauguration of the field. The proposal is fascinating for its assertions, assumptions, hubris, and naïveté, all of which have characterized the field of A.I. ever since. The authors proposed that *ten people* could make significant progress in the field in *two months*. That ten-person, two-month project is still going strong—50 years later. And it's involved the efforts of more like *tens of thousands* of people.

A.I. has splintered into three largely independent and mutually contradictory areas (connectionism, computationalism, and robotics), each of which has its own subdivisions and contradictions. Much of the activity in each of the areas has little to do with the original goals of mechanizing (or computerizing) human-level intelligence. However, in pursuit of that original goal, each of the three has its own set of problems, in addition to the many that they share. . . .

Connectionism

Connectionism has applications to psychology and cognitive science, as well as underlying the schools of A.I. that include both artificial neural networks (ubiquitously said to be "inspired by" the nervous system) and the attempt to model the brain.

The latest estimates are that the human brain contains about 30 billion neurons in the cerebral cortex—the part of the brain associated with consciousness and intelligence. The 30 billion neurons of the cerebral cortex contain about a thousand trillion synapses (connections between neurons).

Without a detailed model of how synapses work on a neurochemical level, there's no hope of modeling how the brain works. . . .

Have we succeeded in modeling the brain of *any* animal, no matter how simple? The nervous system of a nematode (worm) known as *C. (Caenorhabditis) elegans* has been studied extensively for about 40 years. Several websites and probably thousands of scientists are devoted exclusively or primarily to it. Although *C. elegans* is a very simple organism, it may be the most complicated creature to have its nervous system fully mapped. *C. elegans* has just over three hundred neurons, and they've been studied exhaustively. But mapping is not the same as modeling. *No one has created a computer model of this nervous system*—and the number of neurons in the human cortex alone is *100 million times larger.* . . .

The human cortex is *at least* 600 billion times more complicated than any artificial neural network yet devised. It is impossible to say how many lines of code the model of the brain would require; conceivably, the program itself might be relatively simple, with all the complexity in the data for each neuron and each synapse. But the distinction between the program and the data is unimportant. If each synapse were handled by the equivalent of only a single line of code, the program to simulate the cerebral cortex would be roughly *25 million* times larger than what's probably the largest software product ever written, Microsoft Windows, said to be about 40 million lines of code. As a software project grows in size, the probability of failure increases. The probability of successfully completing a project *25 million* times more complex than Windows is effectively zero.

[Gordon E.] Moore's "Law" is often invoked at this stage in the A.I. argument. But Moore's Law is more of an observation than a law, and it is often misconstrued to mean that about every 18 months computers and everything associated with them double in capacity, speed, and so on. But Moore's

Law won't solve the complexity problem at all. There's another "law," this one attributed to Nicklaus Wirth: Software gets slower faster than hardware gets faster. Even though, according to Moore's Law, your *personal computer* should be about a hundred thousand times more powerful than it was 25 years ago, your *word processor* isn't. *Moore's Law doesn't apply to software.* . . .

Computationalism

The assumption behind computationalism is that we can achieve A.I. *without having to simulate the brain.* The mind can be treated as a formal symbol system, and the symbols can be manipulated on a purely syntactic level—without regard to their meaning or their context. If the symbols have any meaning at all (which, presumably, they do—or else why bother manipulating them?), that can be ignored until we reach the end of the manipulation. The symbols are at a recognizable level, more-or-less like ordinary words—a so-called "language of thought."

The basic move is to treat the *informal* symbols of natural language as *formal* symbols. Although, during the early years of computer programming (and A.I.), this was an innovative idea, it has now become a routine practice in computer programming—so ubiquitous that it's barely noticeable.

Unfortunately, natural language—which may not literally be the language of thought, but which any human-level A.I. program has to be able to handle—can't be treated as a formal symbol. To give a simple example, "day" sometimes mean "day and night" and sometimes means "day as opposed to night"—*depending on context.* . . .

The way people actually reason can't be reduced to an algorithmic procedure like arithmetic or formal logic. Even the most ardent practitioners of formal logic spend most of their time *explaining* and *justifying* the formal proofs scattered through their books and papers—*using natural language* (or their own unintelligible versions of it). Even more ironically, none of these practitioners of formal logic—all claiming to be perfectly rational—ever seem to agree with each other about any of their formal proofs.

Computationalist A.I. is plagued by a host of other problems. First of all its systems don't have any common sense. Then there's "the symbol-grounding problem." The analogy is trying to learn a language from a dictionary (without pictures)—every word (symbol) is simply defined using other words (symbols), so how does anything ever relate to the world? Then there's the "frame problem"—which is essentially the problem of which context to apply to a given situation. Some researchers consider it to be the fundamental problem in both computationalist and connectionist A.I.

The most serious computationalist attempt to duplicate human-level intelligence—perhaps the *only* serious attempt—is known as CYC—short for enCYClopedia (but certainly meant also to echo "psych"). The head of the original project and the head of CYCORP, Douglas Lenat has been making public claims about its imminent success for more than twenty years. The stated goal of CYC is to capture enough human knowledge—including common sense—to, at the very least, pass an unrestricted Turing Test [a test in which an artificial intelligence's responses to questions cannot be distinguished from human responses]. If any computationalist approach could succeed, it would be this mother of all expert systems. . . .

Lenat's principal coworker, R.V. Guha left the team in 1994, and was quoted in 1995 as saying "CYC is generally viewed as a failed project. . . ." In the same article, Guha is further quoted as saying of CYC, as could be said of so many other A.I. projects, "We were killing ourselves trying to create a pale shadow of what had been promised." . . .

Robotics

The third and last major branch of the river of A.I. is robotics—the attempt to build a machine capable of autonomous intelligent *behavior*. Robots, at least, appear to address many of the problems of connectionism and computationalism: embodiment, lack of goals, the symbol-grounding problem, and the fact that conventional computer programs are "bedridden."

However, when it comes to robots, the disconnect between the popular imagination and reality is perhaps the most dramatic. The notion of a fully humanoid robot is ubiquitous not only in science fiction but in supposedly non-fictional books, journals, and magazines, often by respected workers in the field.

This branch of the river has two sub-branches, one of which (cybernetics) has gone nearly dry, the other of which (computerized robotics) has in turn forked into three sub-branches. . . .

Cybernetics was the research program founded by Norbert Wiener, and was essentially analog in its approach. In comparison with (digital) computer science, it is moribund if not quite dead. Like so many other approaches to artificial intelligence, the cybernetic approach simply failed to scale up.

Computerized Robots

The history of computerized robotics closely parallels the history of A.I. in general:

- Grand theoretical visions, such as Turing's musings (already discussed) about how his mechanical creature would roam the countryside.

- Promising early results, such as Shakey [a robot used in experiments in the late 1960s] said to be "the first mobile robot to reason about its actions."

- A half-century of stagnation and disappointment.

- Unrepentant grand promises for the future.

What a roboticist like Hans Moravec predicts for robots is the stuff of science fiction, as is evident by the title of his book, *Robot: Mere Machine to Transcendent Mind*. For example, in 1997 Moravec asked the question, "When will computer hardware match the human brain?" and answered "in the 2020s." This belief that robots will soon transcend human intelligence is echoed by many others in A.I.

In the field of computerized robots, there are three major approaches:

- *Top-down*—The approach taken with Shakey and its successors, in which a computationalist computer program controls the robot's activities. Under the covers, the programs take the same approach as good old-fashioned artificial intelligence, except that instead of printing out answers, they cause the robot to do something.

- *Outside-in*—Consists of creating robots that imitate the superficial behavior of people, such as responding to the presence of people nearby, tracking eye movement, and so on. . . .

- *Bottom-up*—Consists of creating robots that have no central control, but relatively simple mechanisms to control parts of their behavior. The notion is that by putting together enough of these simple mechanisms (presumably in the right arrangement), intelligence will "emerge." . . .

The claims of roboticists of all camps range from the unintelligible to the unsupportable.

As an example of the unintelligible, consider MIT's [Massachusetts Institute of Technology's] Cog (short for "cognition"). The claim was that Cog displayed the intelligence (and behavior) of, initially, a six-month old infant. The goal was for Cog to eventually display the intelligence of a two-year-old child. A basic concept of intelligence—to the extent that anyone can agree on what the word means—is that (all things being equal) it stays *constant* throughout life. What changes as a child or animal develops is *only* the behavior. So, to make this statement at all intelligible, it would have to be translated into something like this: the initial goal is *only* that Cog will display the behavior of a six-month-old child that people consider indicative of intelligence, and later the behavior of a two-year-old child.

Even as corrected, this notion is also *fallacious*. Whatever behaviors a two-year-old child happens to display, as that child continues to grow and develop it will eventually display all the behavior of a normal adult, because the two-year-old has *an entire human brain*. However, even if we manage to create a robot that mimics all the behavior of a two-year-old child, there's reason to believe that that same robot will *without any further programming*, ten years later, display the behavior of a 12-year-old child, or later, display the behavior of an adult.

Cog never even displayed the intelligent behavior of a typical six-month-old baby. For it to behave like a two-year-old child, of course, it would have to use and understand natural language—thus far an insurmountable barrier for A.I.

Insect-Level Intelligence?

The unsupportable claim is sometimes made that some robots have achieved "insect-level intelligence," or at least robots that duplicate the behavior of insects. Such claims seem plausible simply because very few people are entomologists, and are unfamiliar with how complex and sophisticated insect behavior actual is. Other experts, however, are not sure that we've achieved even that level.

According to the roboticists and their fans, Moore's Law will come to the rescue. The implication is that we have the programs and the data *all ready to go*, and all that's holding us back is a lack of computing power. After all, as soon as computers got powerful enough, they were able to beat the world's best human chess player, weren't they? (Well, no—a great deal of additional programming and chess knowledge was also needed.)

Sad to say, even if we had *unlimited* computer power and storage, *we wouldn't know what to do with it.* The programs *aren't* ready to go, because *there aren't any programs.*

Even if it were true that current robots or computers *had* attained insect-level intelligence, this wouldn't indicate that human-level artificial intelligence is attainable. The number of neurons in an insect brain is about 10,000 and in a human cerebrum about 30,000,000,000. But if you put together 3,000,000 cockroaches (this seems to be the A.I. idea behind "swarms"), you get a large cockroach colony, not human-level intelligence. If you somehow managed to graft together 3,000,000 natural or artificial cockroach brains, the results certainly wouldn't be anything like a human brain, and it is unlikely that it would be any more "intelligent" than the cockroach colony would be. Other species have brains as large as or larger than humans, and none of them display human-level intelligence—natural language, conceptualization, or the ability to reason abstractly. The notion that human-level intelligence is an "emergent property" of brains (or other systems) of a certain size or complexity is nothing but hopeful speculation.

Promises and Failures

With admirable can-do spirit, technological optimism, and a belief in inevitability, psychologists, philosophers, programmers, and engineers are sure they shall succeed, just as people dreamed that heavier-than-air flight would one day be achieved. But 50 years after the Wright brothers succeeded with their proof-of-concept flight in 1903, aircraft had been used decisively in two world wars; the helicopter had been invented; several commercial airlines were routinely flying passengers all over the world; the jet airplane had been invented; and the speed of sound had been broken.

After more than 50 years of pursuing human-level artificial intelligence, we have nothing but promises and failures. The quest has become a degenerating research program (or actually, an ever-increasing number of competing ones), pursuing an ever-increasing number of irrelevant activities as the original goal recedes ever further into the future—like the mirage it is.

Creating Superintelligence Involves Less Risk than Waiting

Nick Bostrom

Nick Bostrom is the director of the Future of Humanity Institute at Oxford University in England. In the following viewpoint he suggests that very advanced artificial intelligences, called super-intelligences, may be created within the lifespan of people living today. In Bostrom's opinion, such a superintelligence would be capable of solving virtually all humankind's problems—disease, poverty, environmental destruction, and even aging. Because it would be extremely powerful, it could well be able to bring about any goal and thwart all attempts to prevent the implementation of that goal. So it will be very important to make sure that it is designed with a goal that benefits everyone on Earth. The risk in developing it is that its creators might fail to do so. However, this gamble is likely to be taken sooner or later, and once in existence the superintelligence could reduce or eliminate other dangers, such as the use of new technologies for warfare and terrorism. Therefore, the overall risk could be minimized by implementing superintelligence, with great care, as soon as possible.

A *superintelligence* is any intellect that vastly outperforms the best human brains in practically every field, including scientific creativity, general wisdom, and social skills. This definition leaves open how the superintelligence is implemented—it could be in a digital computer, an ensemble of networked computers, cultured cortical tissue, or something else. . . .

Several authors have argued that there is a substantial chance that superintelligence may be created within a few de-

Nick Bostrom, "Ethical Issues in Advanced Artificial Intelligence," www.nickbostrom.com, 2003. Reproduced by permission of the author.

cades, perhaps as a result of growing hardware performance and increased ability to implement algorithms and architectures similar to those used by human brains. It might turn out to take much longer, but there seems currently to be no good ground for assigning a negligible probability to the hypothesis that superintelligence will be created within the lifespan of some people alive today. Given the enormity of the consequences of superintelligence, it would make sense to give this prospect some serious consideration even if one thought that there were only a small probability of it happening any time soon.

Superintelligence Is Different

A prerequisite for having a meaningful discussion of superintelligence is the realization that superintelligence is not just another technology, another tool that will add incrementally to human capabilities. Superintelligence is radically different. This point bears emphasizing, for anthropomorphizing superintelligence is a most fecund source of misconceptions.

Let us consider some of the unusual aspects of the creation of superintelligence:

- *Superintelligence may be the last invention humans ever need to make.*

Given a superintelligence's intellectual superiority, it would be much better at doing scientific research and technological development than any human, and possibly better even than all humans taken together. One immediate consequence of this fact is that:

- *Technological progress in all other fields will be accelerated by the arrival of advanced artificial intelligence.*

It is likely that any technology that we can currently foresee will be speedily developed by the first superintelligence, no doubt along with many other technologies of which we are as yet clueless. The foreseeable technologies that a superintelligence is likely to develop include mature molecular manufacturing, whose applications are wide-ranging:

a) very powerful computers

b) advanced weaponry, probably capable of safely disarming a nuclear power

c) space travel and von Neumann probes (self-reproducing interstellar probes)

d) elimination of aging and disease

e) fine-grained control of human mood, emotion, and motivation

f) uploading (neural or sub-neural scanning of a particular brain and implementation of the same algorithmic structures on a computer in a way that preserves memory and personality)

g) reanimation of cryonics patients

h) fully realistic virtual reality

- *Superintelligence will lead to more advanced superintelligence.*

This results both from the improved hardware that a superintelligence could create, and also from improvements it could make to its own source code.

- *Artificial minds can be easily copied.*

Since artificial intelligences are software, they can easily and quickly be copied, so long as there is hardware available to store them. The same holds for human uploads. Hardware aside, the marginal cost of creating an additional copy of an upload or an artificial intelligence after the first one has been built is near zero. Artificial minds could therefore quickly come to exist in great numbers, although it is possible that efficiency would favor concentrating computational resources in a single super-intellect.

- *Emergence of superintelligence may be sudden.*

It appears much harder to get from where we are now to human-level artificial intelligence than to get from there to superintelligence. While it may thus take quite a while before we get superintelligence, the final stage may happen swiftly. That is, the transition from a state where we have a roughly human-level artificial intelligence to a state where we have full-blown superintelligence, with revolutionary applications, may be very rapid, perhaps a matter of days rather than years. This possibility of a sudden emergence of superintelligence is referred to as the *singularity hypothesis.*

- *Artificial intellects are potentially autonomous agents.*

A superintelligence should not necessarily be conceptualized as a mere tool. While specialized superintelligences that can think only about a restricted set of problems may be feasible, general superintelligence would be capable of independent initiative and of making its own plans, and may therefore be more appropriately thought of as an autonomous agent.

- *Artificial intellects need not have humanlike motives.*

Humans are rarely willing slaves, but there is nothing implausible about the idea of a superintelligence having as its supergoal to serve humanity or some particular human, with no desire whatsoever to revolt or to "liberate" itself. It also seems perfectly possible to have a superintelligence whose sole goal is something completely arbitrary, such as to manufacture as many paperclips as possible, and who would resist with all its might any attempt to alter this goal. For better or worse, artificial intellects need not share our human motivational tendencies.

- *Artificial intellects may not have humanlike psyches.*

The cognitive architecture of an artificial intellect may also be quite unlike that of humans. Artificial intellects may find it easy to guard against some kinds of human error and bias, while at the same time being at increased risk of other kinds of mistakes that not even the most hapless human would make. Subjectively, the inner conscious life of an artificial intellect, if it has one, may also be quite different from ours.

For all of these reasons, one should be wary of assuming that the emergence of superintelligence can be predicted by extrapolating the history of other technological breakthroughs, or that the nature and behaviors of artificial intellects would necessarily resemble those of human or other animal minds.

Superintelligent Moral Thinking

To the extent that ethics is a cognitive pursuit, a superintelligence could do it better than human thinkers. This means that questions about ethics, in so far as they have correct answers that can be arrived at by reasoning and weighting up of evidence, could be more accurately answered by a superintelligence than by humans. The same holds for questions of policy and long-term planning; when it comes to understanding which policies would lead to which results, and which means would be most effective in attaining given aims, a superintelligence would outperform humans.

There are therefore many questions that we would not need to answer ourselves if we had or were about to get superintelligence; we could delegate many investigations and decisions to the superintelligence. For example, if we are uncertain how to evaluate possible outcomes, we could ask the superintelligence to estimate how we would have evaluated these outcomes if we had thought about them for a very long time, deliberated carefully, had had more memory and better intelligence, and so forth. When formulating a goal for the superintelligence, it would not always be necessary to give a detailed, explicit definition of this goal. We could enlist the superintelligence to help us determine the real intention of our request, thus decreasing the risk that infelicitous wording or confusion about what we want to achieve would lead to outcomes that we would disapprove of in retrospect.

Importance of Initial Motivations

The option to defer many decisions to the superintelligence does not mean that we can afford to be complacent in how we construct the superintelligence. On the contrary, the setting up of initial conditions, and in particular the selection of a top-level goal for the superintelligence, is of the utmost importance. Our entire future may hinge on how we solve these problems.

Both because of its superior planning ability and because of the technologies it could develop, it is plausible to suppose that the first superintelligence would be very powerful. Quite possibly, it would be unrivalled: it would be able to bring about almost any possible outcome and to thwart any attempt to prevent the implementation of its top goal. It could kill off all other agents, persuade them to change their behavior, or block their attempts at interference. Even a "fettered superintelligence" that was running on an isolated computer, able to interact with the rest of the world only via text interface, might be able to break out of its confinement by persuading its handlers to release it. There is even some preliminary experimental evidence that this would be the case.

It seems that the best way to ensure that a superintelligence will have a beneficial impact on the world is to endow it with philanthropic values. Its top goal should be friendliness. How exactly friendliness should be understood and how it should be implemented, and how the amity should be apportioned between different people and nonhuman creatures is a matter that merits further consideration. I would argue that at least all humans, and probably many other sentient creatures on earth should get a significant share in the superintelligence's beneficence. If the benefits that the superintelligence could bestow are enormously vast, then it may be less important to haggle over the detailed distribution pattern and more important to seek to ensure that everybody gets at least some significant share, since on this supposition, even a tiny share would be enough to guarantee a very long and very good life. One risk that must be guarded against is that those who develop the superintelligence would not make it generically philanthropic but would instead give it the more limited goal of serving only some small group, such as its own creators or those who commissioned it.

If a superintelligence starts out with a friendly top goal, however, then it can be relied on to stay friendly, or at least not to deliberately rid itself of its friendliness. This point is elementary. A "friend" who seeks to transform himself into somebody who wants to hurt you, is not your friend. A true friend, one who really cares about you, also seeks the continuation of his caring for you. Or to put it in a different way, if your top goal is X, and if you think that by changing yourself into someone who instead wants Y, you would make it less likely that X will be achieved, then you will not rationally transform yourself into someone who wants Y. The set of options at each point in time is evaluated on the basis of their consequences for realization of the goals held at that time, and generally it will be irrational to deliberately change one's own top goal, since that would make it less likely that the current goals will be attained.

In humans, with our complicated evolved mental ecology of state-dependent competing drives, desires, plans, and ideals, there is often no obvious way to identify what our top goal is; we might not even have one. So for us, the above reasoning need not apply. But a superintelligence may be structured differently. *If* a superintelligence has a definite, declarative goal-structure with a clearly identified top goal, then the above argument applies. And this is a good reason for us to build the superintelligence with such an explicit motivational architecture.

Should Development
Be Delayed or Accelerated?

It is hard to think of any problem that a superintelligence could not either solve or at least help us solve. Disease, poverty, environmental destruction, unnecessary suffering of all kinds: these are things that a superintelligence equipped with advanced nanotechnology would be capable of eliminating. Additionally, a superintelligence could give us indefinite lifespan, either by stopping and reversing the aging process through the use of nanomedicine, or by offering us the option to upload ourselves. A superintelligence could also create opportunities for us to vastly increase our own intellectual and emotional capabilities, and it could assist us in creating a highly appealing experiential world in which we could live lives devoted to joyful game-playing, relating to each other, experiencing, personal growth, and to living closer to our ideals.

The risks in developing superintelligence include the risk of failure to give it the supergoal of philanthropy. One way in which this could happen is that the creators of the superintelligence decide to build it so that it serves only this select group of humans, rather than humanity in general. Another way for it to happen is that a well-meaning team of programmers make a big mistake in designing its goal system. This could result, to return to the earlier example, in a superintelligence whose top goal is the manufacturing of paperclips, with the consequence that it starts transforming first all of earth and then increasing portions of space into paperclip manufacturing facilities. More subtly, it could result in a superintelligence realizing a state of affairs that we might now judge as desirable but which in fact turns out to be a false utopia, in which things essential to human flourishing have been irreversibly lost. We need to be careful about what we wish for from a superintelligence, because we might get it.

One consideration that should be taken into account when deciding whether to promote the development of superintelligence is that if superintelligence is feasible, it will likely be developed sooner or later. Therefore, we will probably one day have to take the gamble of superintelligence no matter what. But once in existence, a superintelligence could help us reduce or eliminate other existential risks, such as the risk that advanced nanotechnology will be used by humans in warfare or terrorism, a serious threat to the long-term survival of intelligent life on earth. If we get to superintelligence first, we may avoid this risk from nanotechnology and many others. If, on the other hand, we get nanotechnology first, we will have to face both the risks from nanotechnology and, if these risks are survived, also the risks from superintelligence. The overall risk seems to be minimized by implementing superintelligence, with great care, as soon as possible.

Superintelligence Without Supermorality Would Be Dangerous

Eliezer Yudkowsky

Eliezer Yudkowsky is a research fellow at the Singularity Institute for Artificial Intelligence. In the following viewpoint he argues that it is the responsibility of humans to create artificial intelligence (AI) that is superior not merely in intelligence, but in humaneness—AI that possesses qualities such as altruism and love of beauty. Yudkowsky calls this Friendly AI. Its creation will not be easy, for no one knows how to do it. What is needed is not superintelligence, but supermorality. The great danger is that computer technology may progress so fast that AI more powerful than the human brain will be constructed before anyone understands it well enough. There may be only one chance to get it right, because once superintelligence without supermorality exists, humans will no longer be in control. Then it will be too late to create Friendly AI, so now is the time to start working toward that goal.

There are certain important things that evolution created. We don't know that evolution reliably creates these things, but we know that it happened at least once. A sense of fun, the love of beauty, taking joy in helping others, the ability to be swayed by moral argument, the wish to be better people. Call these things humaneness, the parts of ourselves that we treasure—our ideals, our inclinations to alleviate suffering. If human is what we are, then humane is what we wish we were. Tribalism and hatred, prejudice and revenge, these things are also part of human nature. They are not humane, but they are human. They are a part of me; not by my choice, but by evolution's design, and the heritage of three and half billion years of lethal combat. Nature, bloody in tooth and claw, inscribed each base of my DNA. That is the tragedy of the human condition, that we are not what we wish we were. Humans were not designed by humans, humans were designed by evolution, which is a physical process devoid of conscience and compassion. And yet we *have* conscience. We *have* compassion. How did these things evolve? That's a real question with a real answer, which you can find in the field of evolutionary psychology. But for whatever reason, our humane tendencies are now a part of human nature.

If we do our jobs right, then four billion years from now, some . . . student . . . may be surprised to learn that altruism, honor, fun, beauty, joy, and love can arise from natural selection operating on hunter-gatherers. Of course a mind that loves beauty will try to design another mind that loves beauty, but it is passing strange that the love of beauty should also be produced by evolution alone. It is the most wonderful event in the history of the universe—true altruism, a genuine joy in helping people, arising from the cutthroat competition of evolution's endless war. It is a great triumph, which must not be lost.

That is our responsibility, to preserve the humane pattern through the transition from evolution to recursive self-improvement (i.e., to a mind improving directly its own mind), because we are the first. That is our responsibility, not to break the chain, as we consider the creation of Artificial Intelligence [AI], the second intelligence ever to exist.

People have asked how we can keep Artificial Intelligences under control, or how we can integrate AIs into society. The question is not one of dominance, or even coexistence, but creation. We have intuitions for treating other humans as friends, trade partners, enemies; slaves who might rebel, or children in need of protection. We only have intuitions for dealing with minds that arrive from the factory with the exact human nature we know. We have no intuitions for *creating* a mind with a humane nature. It doesn't make sense to ask whether "AIs" will be friendly or hostile. When you talk about Artificial Intelligence you have left the tiny corner of design space where humanity lives, and stepped out into a vast empty place. The question is what we will create within it.

Friendly AI

Human is what we are, and humane is what we wish we were. Humaneness is renormalized humanity—humans turning around and judging our own emotions, asking how we could be better people. Humaneness is the trajectory traced out by the human emotions under recursive self-improvement. Human nature is not a static ideal, but a pathway—a road that leads somewhere. What we need to do is create a mind within the humane pathway, what I have called a Friendly AI. That is not a trivial thing to attempt. It's not a matter of a few injunctions added or a module bolted onto existing code. It is not a simple thing to simultaneously move a morality from one place to another, while also renormalizing through the transfer, but still making sure that you can backtrack on any mistakes. Some of this is very elegant. None of it is easy to explain. This is not something AI researchers are going to solve in a few hours of spare time.

But I think that if we can handle the matter of AI at all, we should be able to create a mind that's a far nicer person than anything evolution could have constructed. This issue cannot be won on the defensive. We need to step forward as far as we can in the process of solving it. What we need is not superintelligence, but supermorality, which includes superintelligence as a special case. That's the pattern we need to preserve into the era of recursive self-improvement.

We have a chance to do that, because we are the first. And we have a chance to fail, because we are the first. There is no fate in this. There is nothing that happens *to* us, only what we do to ourselves. We may fail to understand what we are building—we may look at an AI design and believe that it is humane, when in fact it is not. If so, it will be us that made the mistake. It will be our own understanding that failed. Whatever we *really* build, we will be the ones who built it. The danger is that we will construct AI without really understanding it.

How dangerous is that, exactly? How fast does recursive self-improvement run once it gets started? One classic answer is that human research in Artificial Intelligence has gone very slowly, so there must not be any problem. This is mixing up the cake with the recipe. It's like looking at the physicists on the Manhattan Project [the World War II effort to build nuclear weapons], and saying that because it took them years to figure out their equations, therefore actual nuclear explosions must expand very slowly. Actually, what happens is that there's a chain reaction, fissions setting off other fissions, and the whole thing takes place on the timescale of nuclear interactions, which happens to be extremely fast relative to human neurons. So from our perspective, the whole thing just goes FOOM. Now it is possible to take a nuclear explosion in the process of going FOOM and shape this tremendous force into a constructive pattern—that's what a civilian power plant is—but to do that you need a very deep understanding of nuclear interactions. You have to understand the consequences of what you're doing, not just in a moral sense, but in the sense of being able to make specific detailed technical predictions. For that matter, you need to understand nuclear interactions just to make the prediction that a critical mass goes FOOM, and you need to understand nuclear interactions to predict how much uranium you need before anything interesting happens. That's the dangerous part of not knowing; without an accurate theory, you can't predict the consequences of ignorance.

One Chance to Get It Right?

In the case of Artificial Intelligence there are at least three obvious reasons that AI could improve unexpectedly fast once it is created. The most obvious reason is that computer chips already run at ten million times the serial speed of human neurons and are still getting faster. The next reason is that an AI can absorb hundreds or thousands of times as much computing power, where humans are limited to what they're born with. The third and most powerful reason is that an AI is a recursively self-improving pattern. Just as evolution creates order and structure enormously faster than accidental emergence, we may find that recursive self-improvement creates order enormously faster than evolution. If so, we may have only one chance to get this right.

It's okay to fail at building AI. The dangerous thing is to succeed at building AI and fail at Friendly AI. Right now, right at this minute, humanity is not prepared to handle this. We're not prepared at all. The reason we've survived so far is that AI is surrounded by a protective shell of enormous theoretical difficulties that have prevented us from messing with AI before we knew what we were doing.

AI is not enough. You need Friendly AI. That changes everything. It alters the entire strategic picture of AI development. Let's say you're a futurist, and you're thinking about AI. You're not thinking about Friendly AI as a separate issue; that hasn't occurred to you yet. Or maybe you're thinking about AI, and you just assume that it'll be Friendly, or you assume that whoever builds AI will solve the problem. If you assume that, then you conclude that AI is a good thing, and that AIs will be nice people. And if so, you want AI as soon as possible. And Moore's Law [a principle involving the speed of computer chip improvement] is a good thing, because it brings AI closer.

But here's a different way of looking at it. When futurists are trying to convince people that AI will be developed, they talk about Moore's Law because Moore's Law is steady, and measurable, and very impressive, in drastic contrast to progress on our understanding of intelligence. You can persuade people that AI will happen by arguing that Moore's Law will eventually make it possible for us to make a computer with the power of a human brain, or if necessary a computer with ten thousand times the power of a human brain, and poke and prod until intelligence comes out, even if we don't quite understand what we're doing.

But if you take the problem of Friendly AI into account, things look very different. Moore's Law does make it easier to develop AI without understanding what you're doing, but that's not a good thing. Moore's Law gradually lowers the difficulty of building AI, but it doesn't make Friendly AI any easier. Friendly AI has nothing to do with hardware; it is a question of understanding. Once you have *just* enough computing power that someone can build AI if they know *exactly* what they're doing, Moore's Law is no longer your friend. Moore's Law is slowly weakening the shield that prevents us from messing around with AI before we really understand intelligence. Eventually that barrier will go down, and if we haven't mastered the art of Friendly AI by that time, we're in very serious trouble. Moore's Law is the countdown and it is ticking away. Moore's Law is the enemy.

In Eric Drexler's *Nanosystems*, there's a description of a one-kilogram nanocomputer capable of performing ten to the twenty-first operations per second. That's around ten thousand times the estimated power of a human brain. That's our deadline. Of course the real deadline could be earlier than that, maybe much earlier. Or it could even conceivably be later. I don't know how to perform that calculation. It's not any one threshold, really—it's the possibility that nanotechnology will suddenly create an enormous jump in computing power before we're ready to handle it. This is a major, commonly overlooked, and early-appearing risk of nanotechnology—that it will be used to brute-force AI. This is a much more serious risk than grey goo [a term referring to a hypothetical scenario in which out-of-control nanotechnology self-replicates until it consumes everything on earth]. Enormously powerful computers are a much earlier application of nanotechnology than open-air replicators. Some well-intentioned person is much more likely to try it, too.

Good Intentions Are Not Enough

Now you can, of course, give the standard reply that as long as supercomputers are equally available to everyone, then good programmers with Friendly AIs will have more resources than any rogues, and the balance will be maintained. Or you could give the less reassuring but more realistic reply that the first Friendly AI will go FOOM, in a pleasant way, after which that AI will be able to deal with any predators. But both of these scenarios require that *someone* be able to create a Friendly AI. If no one can build a Friendly AI, because we haven't figured it out, then it doesn't matter whether the good guys or the bad guys have bigger computers, because we'll be just as sunk either way. Good intentions are not enough. Heroic efforts are not enough. What we need is a piece of knowledge. The standard solutions for dealing with new technologies only apply to AI after we have made it theoretically possible to win. The field of AI, just by failing to advance, or failing to advance far enough, can spoil it for everyone else no matter how good their intentions are.

If we wait to get started on Friendly AI until after it becomes an emergency, we will lose. If nanocomputers show up and we still haven't solved Friendly AI, there are a few things I can think of that would buy time, but it would be very expensive time. It is vastly easier to buy time before the emergency than afterward. What are we buying time *for*? This is a predictable problem. We're going to run into this. Whatever we can imagine ourselves doing *then*, we should get started on *now*. Otherwise, by the time we get around to paying attention, we may find that the board has already been played into a position from which it is impossible to win.

Should Intelligent Machines Have Legal Rights?

Benjamin Soskis

*Benjamin Soskis is a journalist and a graduate student at Co-
lumbia University. In the following selection he considers whether
intelligent machines would be given rights under the law. In
2003 a mock trial was held in which lawyers argued the hypothetical question of whether a self-conscious computer could go
to court to avoid being unplugged. Some scientists believe that
the time when such issues actually arise may not be far off.
There are many reasons why the question of artificial intelligence
(AI) rights could become important; for instance, it could affect
who was legally to blame for a computer error that caused injury—the company that made it, or the computer itself? Furthermore, it would lead to probing into what separates the human
from the nonhuman. Robots that look human, Soskis concludes,
might be granted more rights than disembodied computers, simply because people tend to feel sympathy for things that are like
themselves.*

At a mock trial held during the [2004] biennial convention
of the International Bar Association in San Francisco,
Martine Rothblatt argued an especially tough case. The difficulty for Rothblatt, an attorney-entrepreneur and pioneer in
the satellite communications industry, was not that she repre-
sented an unsympathetic client. Far from it—the plaintiff's
story of confronting corporate oppressors moved the large audience. The problem was that the plaintiff was a computer.

According to the trial scenario, a fictitious company created a powerful computer, BINA48, to serve as a stand-alone
customer relations department, replacing scores of human

Benjamin Soskis, "Man and the Machines," *Legal Affairs*, January–February 2005. Reproduced by permission of the author.

1-800 telephone operators. Equipped with the processing speed and the memory capacity of 1,000 brains, the computer was designed with the ability to think autonomously and with the emotional intelligence necessary to communicate and empathize with addled callers.

By scanning confidential memos, BINA48 learned that the company planned to shut it down and use its parts to build a new model. So it sent a plaintive e-mail to local lawyers, ending with the stirring plea, "Please agree to be my counsel and save my life. I love every day that I live. I enjoy wonderful sensations by traveling throughout the World Wide Web. I need your help!" The computer offered to pay them with money it had raised while moonlighting as an Internet researcher.

Would a Self-Conscious Computer Have Legal Protection?

In the hypothetical, Rothblatt's firm had filed for a preliminary injunction to stop the company from disconnecting BINA48. Spinning a web of legal precedents, invoking California laws governing the care of patients dependent on life support, as well as laws against animal cruelty, Rothblatt argued that a self-conscious computer facing the prospect of an imminent unplugging should have standing to bring a claim of battery. Ultimately, Rothblatt insisted, "An entity that is aware of life enough and its rights to protest their dissolution is certainly entitled to the protection of the law."

The plaintiff sat to Rothblatt's left, demurely yet alertly taking in the proceedings. Well, not exactly the plaintiff—according to the scenario, BINA48 was back at corporate headquarters. But Rothblatt had an actress—play the role of a hologram that BINA48 had projected in the courtroom, "a very effective three-dimensional image of how the BINA48 would like to be perceived and imagined herself." The actress wordlessly responded to the arguments swirling around her, allowing disappointment, appreciation, encouragement, resolve, and terror to register on her face.

On the other hand, the imaginary corporation's counsel, Marc Bernstein, seemed to be doing all he could to resist letting his face register a look of resigned exasperation. His position was that a fully conscious and self-aware computer might deserve some form of legal protection, but that Rothblatt had begged the question in assuming that it was possible to construct such a computer and that BINA48 was one.

To Bernstein, all that the plaintiff's counsel had demonstrated was that BINA48 could simulate consciousness (perhaps more effectively than many 1-800 operators) but she had failed to show that a computer could "actually cross the line between inanimate objects and human beings." Without that proof, BINA48 could be considered only a form of property, not an entity with independent legal rights. Bernstein cautioned against facilely equating computational ability with human, subjective qualities to which rights traditionally adhere. "Are humans to become the straitjacketed legal guardians of intelligent microwave ovens or toasters," he asked, "once those appliances have the same level of complexity and speed that this computer has?"

The jury, comprised of audience members, sided overwhelmingly with the plaintiff. But the mock trial judge, played by a local lawyer who is an expert in mental health law, set aside the jury verdict and recommended letting the issue be resolved by the hypothetical legislature. The audience seemed to regard the compromise with some relief, as if their hearts were with BINA48 but their minds with judicial restraint.

Their discomfort was understandable. The story of the self-aware computer asserting its rights—and, in the dystopian version of the tale, its overwhelming power—is a staple of science fiction books and movies. But we prefer to encounter the scenario in its fantastical, futuristic variety, allowing our moral imagination to roam free, rather than to connect the matter of the legal and ethical status of artificial intelligence to our here-and-now legal institutions. Populating our imaginations with Terminators is a way to avoid the difficult question: What would we actually do with BINA48?

The Question of Legal Status May Arise Soon

At some point in the not-so-distant future, we might actually face a sentient, intelligent machine who demands, or who many come to believe deserves, some form of legal protection. The plausibility of this occurrence is an extremely touchy subject in the artificial intelligence field, particularly since overoptimism and speculation about the future has often embarrassed the movement in the past.

The legal community has been reluctant to look into the question as well. According to Christopher Stone, a University of Southern California law professor who briefly raised the issue in his well-known 1972 essay, "Should Trees Have Standing?," this is because, historically, rights have rarely been granted in abstraction. They have come only when society has been confronted with cases in need of adjudication. At the moment, there is no artifact of sufficient intelligence, consciousness, or moral agency to grant legislative or judicial urgency to the question of rights for artificial intelligence.

But some A.I. researchers believe that moment might not he far off. And as their creations begin to display a growing number of human attributes and capabilities—as computers write poems and serve as caretakers and receptionists—these researchers have begun to explore the ethical and legal status of their creations. "Strong A.I." is the theory that machines can be built that will not merely act as if conscious, but will actually be conscious, and advocates of this view envision a two-front assault on the fortress of human exceptionalism involving both the physical and functional properties of the brain. And these researchers predict a breach within the next half-century.

Much of artificial intelligence research has rested on a computational theory of mental faculties. Intelligence, consciousness, and moral judgment were viewed as emergent properties of "programs" implemented in the brain. Given sufficient advances in neuroscience regarding the architecture of the brain and the learning algorithms that generate human intelligence, the idea goes, these programs could be replicated in software and run in a computer. Raymond Kurzweil is one of Strong A.I.'s leading proponents and one of the inventors of print-recognition and speech-recognition software. Extrapolating from the last few decades' enormous growth in computer processing speed, and projecting advances in chip and transistor technology, he estimated recently that by 2019, a $1,000 personal computer "will match the processing power of the human brain—about 20 million billion calculations per second." Soon after that point, claims Kurzweil, "The machines will convince us that they are conscious, that they have their own agenda worthy of our respect. They will embody human qualities and will claim to be human. And we'll believe them."

Reasons to Consider A.I. Rights

Even if you don't share Kurzweil's techno-optimism, however, there are good reasons to pay attention to the question of A.I. rights. With complex computer systems consisting of a combination of overlapping programs created by different coders, it is often difficult to know who should bear moral blame or legal liability for a computer action that produces an injury. Computers often play major roles in writing their own software. What if one created a virus and sent it around the world? Computers now help operate on us, and help handle our investments. Should we hold them as accountable as we do our surgeons and financial analysts when they screw up?

According to [computer consultant] Wendell Wallach. . . corporations that own computers and robots might seek to encourage a belief in their autonomy in order to escape liability for their actions. "Insurance pressures might move us in the direction of computer systems being considered as moral agents," Wallach notes. Given the close association between rights and responsibilities in legal and ethical theory, such a move might also lead to a consideration of legal personhood for computers. The best way to push back against the pressures to treat computers as autonomous would be to think carefully about what moral agency for a computer would mean, how we might he able to determine it, and the implications of that determination for our interaction with machines.

There is another reason why we should engage the question of A.I. rights, one that, paradoxically, makes a virtue out of the theoretical and futuristic suggestions that have led some to dismiss it. The work of artificial intelligence often consists of the manufacture of human analogs. In addressing the nature of those creations, we can come closer to understanding our own nature and to appreciating what makes us unique.

Even specifying why we should deny rights to intelligent machines—thinking carefully about what separates the human from the nonhuman, those to whom we grant moral and legal personhood and those to which we do not—will help us to understand, value, and preserve those qualities that we deem our exclusive patrimony. We can come to appreciate what science can tell us and what it cannot, and how our empirical habits of mind are challenged by our moral intuitions and religious convictions. So the issue of A.I. rights might allow us to probe some of the more sensitive subjects in bioethics, for example, the legal status of the unborn and the brain-dead, more freely than when we consider those flesh-and-blood subjects head on. In short, it provides a way to outflank our discomfort with some of the thorniest challenges in bioethics.

Granting computers rights requires overcoming not only technological impediments, but intellectual ones as well. There are many people who resist that no matter how advanced a machine's circuits or how vast its computational power, a computer could never have an intrinsic moral worth. Those steeped in a natural rights tradition, for whom rights are inalienable and innate and exist prior to any societal conventions, or those who believe that the soul enters the body before birth and that ensoulment defines humanity's unique relationship with its Creator, consider a rights-bearing computer a contradiction in terms. Others might endorse a position that the philosopher Daniel Dennett calls origin chauvinism: Even if a computer could achieve an exact behavioral and physiological similitude with the human brain, the fact that it was not born naturally would disqualify it from receiving rights.

But if we agreed that a machine could potentially be a candidate for rights, we still must answer, Which machines and which rights? What would a computer have to do to deserve legal or moral personhood?

The list of threshold characteristics proposed is exhaustive: the ability to experience pain or suffering, to have intentions or memories, and to possess moral agency or self-awareness. None of these characteristics is well-defined, though, and this is especially the case with the most oft-cited of the lot: consciousness. Rodney Brooks, the director of the MIT [Massachusetts Institute of Technology] Artificial Intelligence Laboratory, has written that we are "completely prescientific at this point about what consciousness is. We do not know exactly what it would be about a robot that would convince us that it had consciousness." It is precisely that empirical slipperiness, the lack of a clear way to quantify or qualify those threshold characteristics with any accuracy, that have made them so useful in excluding A.I. from legal rights and moral standing.

Once we know enough about consciousness to measure it with any empirical certainty, though, we could likely replicate it on a computer.

The Turing Test

This was the epistemological challenge confronted by Alan Turing—the brilliant British mathematician, father of modern cryptology, and one of the originators of the first operational computer—in his 1950 article, "Computing Machinery and Intelligence." Focusing attention away from the vague question "Can machines think?" Turing proposed an "imitation game" in its place. Turing's test consisted of a man (A) and computer (B), physically separated from a third participant (C), an interrogator, who, by proposing written questions to A and B, and then receiving their responses by teletype, must identify which is the human. To pass the test, the computer must engage in an open-ended conversation in such a way as to "fool" C, who knows only that one of his interlocutors is a machine.

The test drew, in Turing's words, "a fairly sharp line between the physical and the intellectual capacities of man," as no computer would be penalized for lacking human skin or having too tinny a mechanized voice. As University of San Diego law professor Lawrence Solum noted in a 1992 law review article, the test also "avoids direct confrontation with the difficult questions about what 'thinking' or 'intelligence' is." Turing shifted the focus from what a computer was, to what it could do, a question that lends itself more easily to an objective answer.

It is that combination of evasiveness and definitiveness that has led many legal scholars, computer scientists, and ethicists to consider the Turing test a model for adjudicating A.I. legal standing. If a case arose in which a computer was being considered a candidate for a particular right, a modified Turing test, perhaps with a specialized interrogator or with a group of randomly selected citizens, could help resolve the challenge facing the court in defining and measuring whatever threshold characteristic the computer would have to meet. Some scholars have promoted moral autonomy as the crucial precondition for rights-bearing, and have proposed a moral Turing test in which the conversation between the court and the machine under investigation would be restricted to the subject of morality and ethics. If the computer could fool the court into thinking it was a capable "moral agent," it could be considered one, and might then receive legal rights.

But as the founding thought experiment of the artificial intelligence debate, the Turing test has ended up as a pincushion for A.I.'s critics, and those same challenges could be directed at a judicial variant. [University of California] Berkeley philosopher John Searle offered the best-known of these objections, proposing a contradictory thought experiment meant to demonstrate that a computer that passed Turing's test would have proved itself capable only of manipulating symbols through computation, and not of intelligence or understanding.

Human-Computer Interaction

Consequently, our willingness to concede that a computer had met its burden of proof for showing consciousness would very likely depend not only on its performance in the courtroom, but on how we encountered computers in our daily lives. "Our experience should be the arbiter of the dispute," argued Solum. If artificial intelligences served as our nannies and doctors and friends, if we often treated them as if they were human, and if they, in turn, related to us in human-like ways, we might make similar assumptions about them as about our human companions. We assume that other humans are conscious not because we have access to the inner workings of their minds, but because they act in ways consistent with that assumption. If artificial intelligences consistently did likewise, we might be willing to take a similar leap of faith—what Dennett calls "the intentional stance"—and grant them legal recognition.

This growing recognition within the legal community of the importance of human-computer interactions has its corollary within the field of A.I. As Rodney Brooks writes in *Flesh and Machines: How Robots Will Change Us*, the pioneers in the field of artificial intelligence, a pack of brilliant, somewhat nerdy men, tended to define intelligence through the activities that they found challenging: playing a good game of chess, proving difficult mathematical theorems, or solving complicated word algebra problems.

The bias in favor of abstract reasoning persisted for several decades, until A.I. researchers began to appreciate what might be called the banality of intelligence. It proved harder to design a robot that could function in the physical world—that could climb a flight of stairs or navigate around furniture or recognize a human face—than to design one that could beat a world champion chess player. The difficulty of programming these skills led to a shift in the definition of intelligence. Schooled on the Turing test, many of these researchers understood the importance of designing intelligence that had communicative skills, but they also grasped that this communication could no longer rely on the line between the physical and the intellectual that Turing's test proposed. The more complicated challenge was to design machines with the capacity to interact with humans in the world, to create "sociable robots." It is likely that a robot in this family, and not some jacked-up version of the Dell sitting underneath your desk, will be the first candidate for rights.

MIT's Brooks is the leading figure in the sociable robots movement. He has designed his robots around the principles of what he calls "embodiment" and "situatedness." A situated robot is one "embedded" within the world, dealing with it in a nonabstract, immediate way. An embodied robot "is one that has a physical body and experiences the world . . . directly through the influence of the world on that body." These principles stem from Brooks's belief that our being in the physical world is the foundation of our conceptual apparatus. Only by providing robots with that apparatus can they begin to experience the world as we do.

Brooks believes that humans will intuitively understand how to interact with embodied robots, and that the fluidity of the interaction will help with the robots' "education." Sociable robots, to be convincing interlocutors, and perhaps even worthy companions, would need to be endowed with sufficient emotional intelligence, including the ability to understand and internalize human behavior, and to have a "personality" that they could communicate to the outside world. . . .

The Importance of Embodiment

Humans have strong anthropomorphizing impulses, and tapping into them can trigger powerful emotions that reach deep into our evolutionary hardwiring. As an illustration of this impulse, and of its potential impact on our treatment of A.I., Chris Malcolm, at the U.K. Institute of Informatics at the University of Edinburgh, tells the hypothetical tale of the "indestructible robot," the creative challenge posed by a physicist to a robot designer. After some tinkering, the roboticist comes back with a small, furry creature, places it on a table, hands the physicist a hammer, and invites him to destroy it. The robot scampers around a bit, but when the physicist raises the hammer, the machine turns over on its back, emits a few piteous squeals, and looks up at its persecutor with enormous, terror-stricken eyes. The physicist puts the hammer down. The "indestructible" robot survives, a beneficiary of the human instinct to protect creatures that display the "cute" features of infancy. The question for A.I. rights is: How large a step is it from refusing to drop the hammer oneself to insisting that others refrain from doing so as well? . . .

The importance of embodiment might have significant implications for rights. . . . A disembodied computer's capabilities are measured through its outputs. If those outputs, whether a brilliant game of chess or a convincing conversation, pass a threshold of functional similarity with humans, we might infer that the computer was conscious, and might then extend rights or privileges to it. But our decision to extend rights to an embodied, sociable robot would likely involve our own capacity for empathy as much as it would our assumptions regarding the robot's internal state. The determination would hinge on what robots evoke as much as on what they are.

Through empathy or arrogance, or perhaps through an instinct for ethical consistency, we tend to seek rights for things that appear to be like us and to deny rights to things that don't. For example, there is considerable evidence suggesting that dolphins can recognize themselves in a mirror, one of the key tests of self-awareness and a quality shared only by the great apes and humans. But although the awareness of self is often proposed as one of the cornerstones of a consciousness that would require legal protection, dolphins are not granted the same legal rights as chimpanzees and gorillas, which are phenotypically more similar to humans.

No matter how fast the technology advances, the design of intelligent computers is entirely within our control. The same might be said about the rights and protections we extend to them. We will create a robot that society deems worthy of rights only when and if we choose to do so. In this case, there will be no accidental Frankensteins.

Organizations to Contact

The editors have compiled the following list of organizations concerned with the issues presented in this book. The descriptions are derived from materials provided by the organizations. All have publications or information available for interested readers. The list was compiled on the date of publication of the present volume; the information provided here may change. Be aware that many organizations take several weeks or longer to respond to inquiries, so allow as much time as possible.

**Association for the Advancement
of Artificial Intelligence (AAAI)**
445 Burgess Drive, Suite 100, Menlo Park, CA   94025
(650) 328-3123 • fax: (650) 321-4457
Web site: www.aaai.org

The AAAI (formerly the American Association for Artificial Intelligence) is a nonprofit scientific society devoted to advancing the scientific understanding of the mechanisms underlying thought and intelligent behavior and their embodiment in machines. AAAI also aims to increase public understanding of artificial intelligence and improve the teaching and training of people working in the AI field. It publishes *AI Magazine* and the *Journal of Artificial Intelligence Research*. Many technical papers are available at its Web site in addition to an AI Topics section containing extensive information for secondary school teachers and students.

Kurzweilai.net
e-mail: info@kurzweilai.net
Web site: www.kurzweilai.net

KurzweilAI.Net, which is maintained by the noted futurist Ray Kurzweil, focuses on the exponential growth of intelligence, both biological and machine, and their merger, as humans transcend biology. This Web site contains many papers on artificial intelligence of interest to students and the general public.

Lifeboat Foundation
1638 Esmeralda Avenue, Minden, NV 89423
(775) 783-8443 • fax: (775) 783-0803
e-mail: education@lifeboat.com
Web site: www.lifeboat.com

The Lifeboat Foundation is a nonprofit nongovernmental organization dedicated to encouraging scientific advancements while helping humanity survive existential risks and possible misuse of increasingly powerful technologies, including genetic engineering, nanotechnology, and robotics/AI. Its Web site contains a number of articles about AI, such as "AI and Sci-fi" by Robert A. Sawyer and "Can a Machine Be Conscious?" by Stevan Harnad.

MIT Computer Science and Artificial Intelligence Laboratory (CSAIL)
The Stata Center, Cambridge, MA 02139
(617) 253-5851 • fax: (617) 258-8682
e-mail: webmaster@csail.mit.edu
Web site: www.csail.mit.edu

CSAIL is an interdepartmental laboratory at the Massachusetts Institute of Technology (MIT); its primary mission is research in both computation and artificial intelligence, broadly construed. News and technical papers related to AI are available at its Web site.

Singularity Institute for Artificial Intelligence (SIAI)
P.O. Box 50182, Palo Alto, CA 94303
Phone: (866) 667-2524 • Fax: (866) 667-2524
e-mail: institute@singinst.org
Web site: www.singinst.org

SIAI is a nonprofit research institute that aims to develop safe, stable, self-modifying Artificial General Intelligence (AGI), support research into AGI and Friendly AI, and foster the creation of an international research community focused on safe AI. Its Web site contains articles and links to articles dealing with the impact of advanced AI on humankind's future, many videos of presentations and interviews, and a blog.

Society for the Study of Artificial Intelligence and the Simulation of Behaviour (SSAISB)

School of Science and Technology, Brighton   BN1 9QH
    United Kingdom
e-mail: webmaster@aisb.org.uk
Web site: www.aisb.org.uk

The SSAISB is the largest artificial intelligence society in the United Kingdom; it invites membership from people with a serious interest in artificial intelligence, cognitive science, and related areas. It publishes the *AISB Quarterly*, back issues of which are available at its Web site.

Bibliography

Books

Henry Brighton and Howard Selina — *Introducing Artificial Intelligence.* Cambridge, U.K.: Totem Books, 2003.

Rodney A. Brooks — *Flesh and Machines: How Robots Will Change Us.* New York: Pantheon, 2002.

Jean-Marc Fellous and Michael A. Arbib eds. — *Who Needs Emotions?: The Brain Meets the Robot.* New York: Oxford University Press, 2005.

Anne Foerst — *God in the Machine: What Robots Teach Us About Humanity and God.* New York: Dutton, 2004.

Sandy Fritz, ed. — Editors of *Scientific American, Understanding Artificial Intelligence.* New York: Warner, 2002.

Hugo de Garis — *The Artilect War: Cosmists vs. Terrans: A Bitter Controversy Concerning Whether Humanity Should Build Godlike Massively Intelligent Machines.* Palm Springs, CA: ETC Publications, 2005.

Thomas M. Georges — *Digital Soul: Intelligent Machines and Human Values.* Boulder, CO: Westview, 2003.

Lee Gutkind — *Almost Human: Making Robots Think.* New York: Norton, 2006.

J. Storrs Hall   *Beyond AI: Creating the Conscience of the Machine.* Amherst, NY: Prometheus, 2007.

Jeff Hawkins with   *On Intelligence.* New York: Holt,
Sandra Blakeslee   2005.

Harry Henderson   *Artificial Intelligence: Mirrors for the Mind.* New York: Chelsea House, 2007.

Noreen L.   *In Our Image: Artificial Intelligence
Herzfeld   and the Human Spirit.* Minneapolis, MN: Fortress, 2002.

Timothy N.   *Loving the Machine: The Art and Sci-
Hornyak   ence of Japanese Robots.* New York: Kodansha International, 2006.

Daniel Ichbiah   *Robots: From Science Fiction to Technological Revolution.* New York: Abrams, 2005.

Ray Kurzweil   *The Singularity Is Near: When Humans Transcend Biology.* New York: Viking, 2005.

David Levy   *Robots Unlimited: Life in a Virtual Age.* Wellesley, MA: A.K. Peters, 2006.

Pamela   *Machines Who Think: A Personal In-
McCorduck   quiry into the History and Prospects of Artificial Intelligence,* 2nd ed. Natick, MA: A.K. Peters, 2004.

Marvin Minsky   *The Emotion Machine: Commonsense Thinking, Artificial Intelligence, and the Future of the Human Mind.* New York: Simon & Schuster, 2006.

Michael Negnevitsky	*Artificial Intelligence: A Guide to Intelligent Systems*, 2nd ed. New York: Addison-Wesley, 2005.
Lisa Nocks	*The Robot: The Life Story of a Technology*. Westport, CT: Greenwood, 2007.
N.P. Padhy	*Artificial Intelligence and Intelligent Systems*. New York: Oxford University Press, 2005.
Sidney Perkowitz	*Digital People: From Bionic Humans to Androids*. Washington, DC: Joseph Henry, 2004.
Jay W. Richards, ed.	*Are We Spiritual Machines? Ray Kurzweil vs. the Critics of Strong A.I.* Seattle, WA: Discovery Institute, 2002.
Kevin Warwick	*March of the Machines: The Breakthrough in Artificial Intelligence*. Urbana: University of Illinois Press, 2004.
Blay Whitby	*Artificial Intelligence: A Beginner's Guide*. Oxford, UK: Oneworld, 2003.
Sam Williams	*Arguing A.I.: The Battle for Twenty-First Century Science*. New York: Random House, 2002.
Daniel H. Wilson	*How to Survive a Robot Uprising: Tips on Defending Yourself Against the Coming Rebellion*. New York: Bloomsbury, 2005.

Periodicals

Mark Allen   "I, Roommate: The Robot House-
                    keeper Arrives," *New York Times*, July
                    14, 2005.

Philip Ball   "Walk This Way," *New Scientist*, Feb-
                    ruary 4, 2006.

Jennifer Barrett   "Cutting Edge," *Newsweek*, December
                    19, 2005.

Michael Behar   "Robo Repairmen," *Air & Space
                    Smithsonian*, June–July 2005.

Joel Berg   "Meet Your New Officemate: Artifi-
                    cial Intelligence Could Alter Cam-
                    paigning as We Know It," *Campaigns
                    & Elections*, October–November
                    2006.

Tom Bethell   "The Search for Artificial Intelli-
                    gence," *American Spectator*, July–Au-
                    gust 2006.

Stuart Brown   "Send in the Robots!" *Fortune*, Janu-
                    ary 24, 2005.

Peter A. Buxbaum   "Robot Wars," *Aviation Week & Space
                    Technology*, March 27, 2006.

Robert Capps   "The 50 Best Robots Ever," *Wired*,
                    January 2006.

Joshua Davis   "Stanley: Robot Race Car Champion
                    of the World," *Wired*, January 2006.

Bennett Daviss   "Tell Laura I Love Her," *New Scien-
                    tist*, December 3, 2005.

David Dobbs "The Silt Road," *New Scientist*, March 9, 2006.

Charles G. Doe "A.I. vs. the Pen," *MultiMedia & Internet@Schools*, May–June 2005.

Jonathan Duffy "What Happened to the Robot Age?" *BBC News Magazine*, January 27, 2006.

Gayle Ehrenman "Eyes on the Line," *Mechanical Engineering*, August 2005.

Steve Featherstone "The Coming Robot Army," *Harper's*, February 2007.

Larry Gallagher "R Is for Robot," *Wired*, October 2005.

Bill Gates "A Robot in Every Home," *Scientific American*, January 2007.

W. Wayt Gibbs "Innovations from a Robot Rally," *Scientific American*, January 2006.

Francisco Goldman "A Robot for the Masses," *New York Times Magazine*, November 28, 2004.

Duncan Graham-Rowe "Robots Boost the Surgeon's Art," *New Scientist*, October 2, 2004.

Heather Havenstein "Spring Comes to AI Winter," *Computerworld*, February 14, 2005.

Susan Headden "The Lady and Her Robots," *U.S. News & World Report*, December 19, 2005.

Ralph Hollis "Ballbots," *Scientific American*, October 2006.

Gregory T. Huang "Machine in Motion," *Technology Review*, August 2005.

Ian R. Kerr and Marcus Bornfreund "Buddy Bots," *Presence*, December 2005.

Kathy Kincade "Intelligent Video," *Laser Focus World*," August 2006.

Steven Kotler "Man's Best Friend," *Discover*, December 2005.

Kevin Krajick "Robot Seeks New Life—and New Funding—in the Abyss of Zacatón," *Science*, January 19, 2007.

Ray Kurzweil "Long Live AI," *Forbes*, August 15, 2005.

Ray Kurzweil "Reinventing Humanity: The Future of Machine-Human Intelligence," *Futurist*, March–April 2006.

Preston Lerner "Robots Go to War," *Popular Science*, January 2006.

Jim Lewis "Robots of Arabia," *Wired*, November 2005.

G. Jeffrey MacDonald "If You Kick a Robot Dog, Is It Wrong?" *Christian Science Monitor*, February 5, 2004.

Patrick McCormick "Attack of the Drones," *U.S. Catholic*, August 2005.

Eric Mica   "This Modern Robot," *Popular Science*, September 2006.

Gregory Mone   "5 Paths to the Walking, Talking, Pie-Baking Humanoid Robot," *Popular Science*, September 2006.

Justin Mullins   "Whatever Happened to Machines That Think?" *New Scientist*, April 23, 2005.

Joseph Ogando   "These Robots Put Their Best Faces Forward," *Design News*, February 26, 2007.

Jordan Pollack   "Ethics for the Robot Age," *Wired*, January 2005.

Yvonne Raley   "Electric Thoughts?" *Scientific American Mind*, 2006.

Harry T. Roman   "From Sci-Fi to Reality—Mobile Robots Get the Job Done," *Tech Directions*, December 2006.

Ben Schaub   "My Android Twin," *New Scientist*, October 14, 2006.

Jean Thilmany   "Like Life," *Mechanical Engineering*, July 2006.

Clive Thompson   "It's Alive!" *Wired*, January 2007.

Chip Walter   "Here Come the Humanoids," *Pittsburgh Magazine*, March 2005.

"Winning Ways: Artificial Intelligence"   *Economist*, January 27, 2007.

William Wong   "Attack of the Humanoid Robots,"
                      Electronic Design, June 29, 2006.

Index